Coiled Serpent

Poets arising
from the cultural
quakes & shifts
of Los Angeles

EDITED BY Neelanjana Banerjee
Daniel A. Olivas
Ruben J. Rodriguez

TIA CHUCHA PRESS

ISBN: 978-1-882688-52-4

Book Design: Jane Brunette
Cover art: "Coiled Serpent" by Alfonso Aceves

Published by:
Tía Chucha Press
A Project of Tía Chucha's Centro Cultural, Inc.
PO Box 328
San Fernando, CA 91341
tiachucha.org

Distributed by:
Northwestern University Press
Chicago Distribution Center
11030 South Langley Avenue
Chicago IL 60628

Tía Chucha's Centro Cultural & Bookstore is a 501 (c) (3) nonprofit corporation funded in part over the years by the National Endowment for the Arts, California Arts Council, Los Angeles County Arts Commission, Los Angeles Department of Cultural Affairs, The California Community Foundation, the Annenberg Foundation, the Weingart Foundation, the Lia Fund, National Association of Latino Arts and Culture, Ford Foundation, MetLife, Southwest Airlines, the Andy Warhol Foundation for the Visual Arts, the Thrill Hill Foundation, the Middleton Foundation, Center for Cultural Innovation, John Irvine Foundation, Not Just Us Foundation, the Attias Family Foundation, and the Guacamole Fund, among others. Donations have also come from Bruce Springsteen, John Densmore of The Doors, Jackson Browne, Lou Adler, Richard Foos, Gary Stewart, Charles Wright, Adrienne Rich, Tom Hayden, Dave Marsh, Jack Kornfield, Jesus Trevino, David Sandoval, Gary Soto, Denise Chávez and John Randall of the Border Book Festival, Luis & Trini Rodríguez, and others.

Contents

To the life and work of
Watts poet, novelist, essayist, and short story writer
Wanda Coleman

To the Native American poet, activist, sage,
band leader, and movie personality
John Trudell

&

To the great Chicano, indigenous,
and gay man of words and the people
Francisco X. Alarcon

Introduction
City of Angels, City of Poets

...Fire in the village
An energy storm in gathering light
Fire in the village
Changing night a cloud's going to lift
Fire in the village
Liberty is shining in a new world's soul
Fire in the village
The little people listen with a fancy step
Fire in the village
The little people can't help but dance
Fire in the village...

—JOHN TRUDELL

For me, Los Angeles is smoldering, deeply poetic, expansively settled, with rebellion beneath the normalcy, which has *un chingo* to do with our collective and personal spiritual awakenings, creative birthings, political schooling—why our lives are in flames.

This city/village has been rumbling for decades, waking up the world every few years with revolutionary ardor—consider the 1965 Watts Rebellion (now 50 years later), the 1970 Chicano Moratorium Against the Vietnam War (the so-called East L.A. riots), and the 1992 Los Angeles Uprising after the acquittal of police officers in the Rodney King beating—and numerous civil disturbances in between. Close to 100 people killed in these battles and a billion dollars in damage in the 1992 riots alone (with millions more in other conflagrations).

This city has had more civil unrests than any other U.S. city in the past 100 years. L.A. is "shaky town" after all, but this has more to do with social and economic tremors and movements than earthquakes.

Why the title? The coiled serpent is connected to the earth, but also ready to spring, to strike, to defend or to protect. This image appears in various forms in mythologies and walls throughout Asia, Africa, Europe, India, and America. In pre-conquest times, Quetzalcoatl—the Precious Serpent— served as a personification of earth-bound wisdom, the arts and eldership in so-called Meso-America, one of seven "cradles of civilization" that also includes China, Nigeria, Mesopotamia, Egypt, the Indus Valley, and Peru.

As I write this, mostly black and brown people in L.A. are being driven off older urban areas. Witness the gentrification of Echo Park, Highland Park, Pico-Union, Venice, sections of South Central. There's a big 1930 Art Deco building on Broadway downtown where in the early 1980s I rented a space for $60 a month. Today this building has million dollar lofts.

Gentrification, anti-gang injunctions, police violence directed at the poor and working class residents, pushing out the homeless—they are all linked to whether this city, like the state and country, will only benefit the relatively few well-off and powerful rather than those in need.

These social conflicts have an objective foundation: Los Angeles is one of the richest cities in the United States and one of the poorest. What lies beneath all the seething are the social and economic gaps. This is also expressed as gaps in the collective imagination.

This poetry collection addresses the natural and unnatural condition of our city in the first 15 years of the new century: inequalities of income and race, how peace can blossom in a time of perpetual war, the escalation of police killings, and climate peril. These poems are "flower and song"— in xochitl in cuicatl—as the Mexica natives of Mexico would say, stanzas that point the way out of social and personal dilemma by simply being, persisting, even in the in-between spaces, the undefined areas, in the complexities of poetic and mournful pondering of squandered possibilities.

Still we celebrate the native and the immigrant (and so-called immigrants who are actually natives), the queer and straight, women and men, young and old, humanity in all its colors, voices, and fluidity. This book could have been many more hundreds of pages. The limitations of publishing forces us to select one to two poems per poet. We want to publish the best of the poems submitted, not so much for literary acrobatics, but for any wonderment and twists a verse may spring upon a reader.

The backdrop to this collection is a society rent with class, racial, gender, and sexual discord; the foreground is imaginative renderings without limits, without fear. In skilled hands, such poems re-shape the idiom and push our minds to enlarge so they can hold the images. All contribute to the beauty, good, and truth that arise from the ruins, the rages, the desperation beneath every breath. This is about the poet's veracity in challenging "sacred cows": capitalism; the immense powers that control wealth, production, the media; even God and other "precious" things.

How in crisis poems are dreamt, born, fashioned. The world can judge how far these poets have taken this. There is art in the trying.

Currently, I'm Poet Laureate of this contentious, vital, and imaginative city. Over the decades I've read poetry at hundreds of schools, libraries, colleges, universities, graduations, festivals, book fests, juvenile lockups, prisons, bookstores, housing projects, and homeless shelters. I've heard a 14-year-old youth at the Nidorf Juvenile Hall (the largest juvenile lockup in North America) read poetry during a behind-barbed-wire poetry event—at the time, he faced 135 years in prison. I've read poetry with the Homeless Writers Coalition at the El Paso Bar on Main Street (now gone as gentrification encroaches on Skid Row, the largest homeless enclave in the U.S.). I've recited a Nahuatl (a key indigenous tongue of Mexico and Central America) poem at the Hammer Museum to draw attention to the world's "Endangered Languages."

I read poems at the Watts Jazz Festival under the shadow of the Watts Towers with my formerly incarcerated son Ramiro (we lived in Florence and Watts when Ramiro was a baby). I've done months of writing workshops at a Maximum Security yard in Lancaster Prison, the only state prison in L.A. County (although L.A.-area prisoners are 60 percent of the state prison system). I've taken part in a Charles Bukowski Festival in San Pedro and in honor of Wanda Coleman at Leimert Park. Read with John Densmore of the Doors at Hollywood's Montalban Theater and did a one-man poetry-play at the John Anson Ford Theater, directed by the renowned "Funkahuatl," Rubén Guevara. I've read at the Los Angeles Times Festival of Books at UCLA and USC to "Celebrating Words" festivals in the barrios of Sylmar and Pacoima; from the Spanish-language "LeaLA!" book fair in downtown to the "Farce of July" festivals by Xicano Records & Films in Boyle Heights and East L.A. I've even recited love poems with my wife Trini at the Malibu Poetry Series… so many events, too numerous to recall.

From the embattlements, I can see generative ideas, strategies, forms of organization, and meaningful expression toward a fuller, cooperative and creatively active society. We can now envision healthy, thriving, and culturally alive communities for all. And we should embolden ourselves for the long haul struggles until this becomes reality. So here we go, poetry that captures a city, a dreamscape, the shape of land and culture… from its underbelly and from among the unseen and unheard. These are artistic weapons in the social battles upturning what America is today and what it can be—toward a grander sense of belonging and inheritance.

This book is dedicated to the irrepressible African American poet Wanda Coleman, a fiery soul who also embraced and guided many young poets, myself included, a rather raw and hungry writer when we first met some 35 years ago. To John Trudell, the Native American warrior-poet and personal teacher, with whom I spent many hours talking, learning, sharing at his Santa Monica abode soon after I returned from Chicago in 2000. And to my friend and fellow Chicano wordsmith and activist, the much-beloved Francisco X. Alarcon, whose poetry drew from deep in the earth and the bones. All three have passed on, but not their dreams for our humanity, their words, their indelible imprints on countless lives.

The aim again for all of us is to be truly alive, blood flowing, consciously awake, despite death everywhere and our culture stuck in a dying time of archaic ideas, moribund infrastructures, and spirit-crushing forms of control. Poetry takes this challenging time and intertwines it with the relentlessly new, the promise that is yet to be, the impossible become possible.

—*Luis J. Rodriguez, December 2015*

RICARDO LIRA ACUÑA
Intimate Set

so this is an intimate set
between you and me
so please
leave your bags at the door
don't carry what you don't need
come in have a seat
because i want to confess to you
everything
right here
right now
the breakup, the student loans, the days of wine and roses without the
roses, the car crashes, the 40, the 316, the blue bus, the 81, the 84, all of
God's mutated faces on the bus, all the ghosts of you, the days choking on
exhaust and the nights scented of jasmine holding in my guts although I
won't get into every gory detail
i don't want to scare you away
you see it's a new year
a new sun
el sexto sol
a time of transformation
a new me
a new you
and every moment
a snowflake
so you wanna know a secret?
you're free to think for yourself here
you're free to truly be yourself here
you are loved here
because out there
in the *desierto*
and all along that Berlin Wall with Mexico
they can tax us
they can discriminate against us

they can deny us an education, ban our literature and our leaders,
erase our history and our unalienable rights
they can declare war against us
they can invade us
take us hostage and prisoner
poison our water our
food our land our air
they can even shoot and bomb our babies
rape us
sell us
buy us
eat us alive
but they cannot and will not have you
and they cannot and will not have me
and they cannot and will not have this love here
between you and me

THOMAS ADAMS
Breadcrumbs

TO DIANE LUBY LANE, FOUNDER OF GET LIT

She gave us poems,
Dropped them like breadcrumbs
Knowing we couldn't consume them all,
But knowing, too, that one day
We might need them
To find the way back to who we are
Or thought we could be;
Knowing that at some point in life
We all get lost
And seek desperately for clues,
Markers that will lead the way back,
Back to a world that,
As though by divine grace,
Once again makes sense.

She gave us poems,
By Langston and Longfellow,
Baca and Brooks,
Whitman, yes, and even
Shakespeare, as if to show us
That we may think poets dead,
But that they really aren't dead at all,
Just sleeping. Sleeping,
Until the moment we decide
To rise from the dead ourselves,
And wake them up with our ears,
Wake them up so we can listen
To the gift of their words.

She gave us poems,
Poems that speak to us of heartbreak
So we know our broken hearts are not alone,
And that they mend,

And that somehow all that pain
Adds to what we come to know
As beauty, beauty
Which is remembered—
Not the stunning wide-eyed face,
Not the dancer's perfect dimensions,
But rather beauty that transcends
What the eyes in the head
Can see, and opens, instead,
Eyes in the heart.

She gave us poems,
Not just all the informational text
They now tell our teachers to give to us
Under the misinterpreted pretext
That our academic muscles are flexed
Only when we are told "how to,"
Only when we read about what actually exists;
And that writing letters to our congressman counts
While writing poems to our mothers doesn't,
When we know this does little justice to our mothers
Who have always been there—
Even when our congressman wasn't.

She gives us poems,
Dropping them like breadcrumbs
Knowing they are just breadcrumbs,
But knowing, too, that one day
We will need them; that the soul,
Like the mind, gets hungry,
And that when breadcrumbs are all there is,
The best of us will gather them up,
And—with a little imagination,
The right amount of agitation,
Pre-measured intonation
And precisely applied enunciation—
Whip up a resounding meal
That indeed can feed
A starving nation.

She gave us poems.

TANZILA AHMED
Iftar Streets

In the City of Angels,
Where driving into the setting sun
Under the tall shadows of the desert palm fronds
Is this city's absolute icon,
People pray to pavements
Giving *duas* of Road Rage
In cars rushing through
The arteries that give life to this city.
The pink horizon calls my *azaan*.
With my left hand on the steering wheel
My teeth cut into the sweet date
As my right foot steps on the gas pedal speeding for more.
"I should pull over," I think to myself
But in a city where God is invoked in cars, primarily
The wide sky is the dome of my mosque
These roads my prayer rug.
So.
I
Drive
On.

TANZILA AHMED

Haze

Today
Los Angeles smells like India,
Like heavy fog and survival trash burning
Like the thick air
Of dawn and dusk
With almost humidity
And almost dreams
And almost warm at road sides.
It smells dirty
Like struggle
Like life in every suck of breath.
Lungs choke with each deep inhale.
Muscle memories in vertigo
Unsure of where I'm placed.
This smell
Always confusing me with a longing for home
When home is where I stay at.
Here, home is
Smog tinged horizons in hazy yellows and smoky pinks.
Only L.A.'s pollution tinged coastal sunsets
Have 4th dimension colors of epic.
But there,
Smoke us the smell of home
Of *azaan* at *fajir*
And sweaty cold sheets,
Dust coating everything
And trash gets burned for struggled warmth
And death gets burned for serenity in eternity
And here
Smoke is the smell of survival

So maybe
Survival is my solace.
And maybe why the smell of moist smoke is home.

NELSON ALBURQUENQUE
Body Against Me

Why does society use my body against me?
Fat, the American impropriety.

"Large"
     "Lard"
          "Flub"
               "Tub"
     and "Obese"

And yet
 "Brave"
     "Bold"
          "Kind
    and "Divine"

are all words they use to describe the pillars of my mind.

Who of Machinery Beauties is the
one to decide?

Newly pruned,
a peeling fruit,
the unloved body
of a spoiling man.

NELSON ALBURQUENQUE
Eggs on City Limits

I'm getting old,
er.
Ten years ago,
I was 16 and barely
scratching the surface
of my seedling brain.
The stem of my head,
a trunk for my poetry's nest
and its eggs.

But as I strut down
the street, I feel
sad, with emptiness
wallowing in me.
As my feet meet
the curb,
I find
the stains of
yolk
splattered,
like brains
on the road.

The young eggshells
cracked,
crumpled in goo,
new yolk my feet found:
the dreams of an inner youth.

Recipe for a Tattoo

Look for a spot on your skin that you think will do:

Behind the ear for a small, crooked rose
that reminds you of your ex-*novia*.
Along the jawline for the area code of your hood
to let them *vatos* know how *firme* you really are.

Trace the chosen spot with your fingers to show Mamá
where the name of a new lover will be.
Set the timer for how many times she shakes her head and calls you a *mensa*.

Separately mix the *amarillos, azules,* and black inks
'til well blended and test it like you would
a can of spray paint on the side wall of your *vecino's* house.

Place your tongue on an ounce of *chiles rojos.*
Power your electric needle.
Intensity: *bien chingón.*

Stare into the sun for thirty seconds. *No llores.*

Apply ice on the cherry blossoms along your ankle,
swollen like bruised plums after stumbling on heels
during a night at the bar with the *cuatas.*

Gaze at the heart tattoo on your ring finger
         smudged during a three-month engagement,
                  a kiss behind a grimy East L.A. chapel on 1st Street.

Cut three leaves of *yerba buena* from the yard and rub on the eyes until dry.
Mix a teaspoon of *limón* with a shot of tequila.
Drink it.

You said you'd never get the L.A symbol
but you get not one but two *porque*... why not?
Go Dodgers.
You remember how you swore to *Diosito*
how you wouldn't get any skulls on your arms either
(well, at least some have flowers, mom).

Preheat any regret to 400 degrees, depending on the thickness.
Take a shot of tequila and consider another long-term commitment.
Repeat from step one.

LI YUN ALVARADO
In Los Angeles

I watch the morning traffic report
to learn my new geography.

Traffic. More of an adjective
than noun in these parts.

How did you get here? *Traffic.*
How close are you? *Traffic.*
How are you doing? *Traffic!!*

Despite stares, suspicion,
I walk. Tap Card
in back pocket,

I walk.

When it comes to weapons
on wheels, I'd rather not
pull the trigger myself.

MELISSA F. ALVARADO
Fifth Grade

In the fifth grade, when the teacher asked us
to raise our hands if we thought we would be
smokers when we grew up,
I raised my hand.
In the fifth grade Mrs. Stall took away
my whole box of erasers that I wouldn't dare
use to erase. Instead
I would smell them, one by one, and then
I would line them up in a row on my desk
deciding if I would let Amy or Sara
borrow one for the day, just to hold and smell,
as if they were given an award for best of show
from the golden box that held an eraser
shaped like a grape, one shaped like a strawberry,
and one like a banana.
I had ordered them from an insert from
the *Weekly Reader* Mrs. Stall gave us. So I didn't see the big deal
when the eraser that was shaped like an orange
rolled all the way from my desk in the back row
to the front of the room where it banged into her pointy shoes
like they were two little bowling pins.

KARINA OLIVA ALVARADO

By the Tree

The young man wakes
He had slept, curled at the trunk
of a tree growing on the only piece
of dirt found between concrete

He had tried to sleep
under a torn and thin midnight
with a bottled
paper bag cradled by his heart,
tucked underneath his shirt

The concrete shows traces
of last night's battle
speckled splatter with vomit
from within so young, alone

He yells at the air, as if
at the mocking face of the sun: *ffa-khew*
with rattle in his throat, a swoosh
of seeds of the gourd of the Quiche
language that betrays him
like teeth knocked out with one
swift punch

He tried to drop
all memory of a world where *quetzales* wrote
on skies with emerald feathers
words left floating like his name

Fa-khew to forget with a bite of his tongue
to forget he had known how to dream
searching
patting his pockets to find

and chew a mint stick of gum
like the English he carries in his jean pocket
for a hard morning
just like this one

RAFAEL F J ALVARADO

Untitled Prison Poem, #30

last night as some inmates
pounded their cells at twelve
I thought to myself
at least there are
a few less guns
being shot in the air this year

E. AMATO

Earthquake Weather

the hummingbirds are bold
the crows preoccupied with lust
marine layer blankets coast
inland temperatures are triple digits
and you are the answer to everything

this must be earthquake weather
the sideways before the upside down
the aberration before the landslide
in regular weather
hummingbirds are shy
crows sharpen for next meal
temperatures differ barely ten degrees
and I am my only answer to everything

it's hard to be afraid of earthquakes
you never know when they will come
'earthquake weather' we say
like we are seismographically sensitive
instead of confused weather vanes

if you are my answer to everything
questions reframe houses rebuild from foundation
tsunamis coax into bottles by kind word
if you are my answer it is earthquake weather
seismic sensors shift to scared—

we can't be afraid of earthquakes
so much as prepare for them
filling in cracks finding stress points
anticipating shattering change—
even solids can be liquid
in the right conditions

if your touch reaches me tremble
shivers across all of my faults
each one shaken then thrust
forever deep in a forgetful core
I know now there will be an instant
that will feel like forever
when you will earthquake through me
creating entirely unforeseen landscape

WILLIAM ARCHILA
Three Minutes with Mingus

When I read of poets & their lives,
  son of a milkman & seamstress, raised
in a whistle-stop town or village, a child
  who spent his after-school hours deep
in the pages of a library book, I want to go
  back to my childhood, back to the war,
rescue that boy under the bed, listening
  to what bullets can do to a man, take him
out of the homeland, enroll him in school,
  his class-size ten, unfold the fables
of the sea, a Spanish galleon slamming up
  & down the high waters. This is why
I write poems, why I prefer solitude
  when I listen to your lazy sound
of brass on the phonograph. You give
  language to black roosters & fossil bones,
break down phrases between the LA River
  & the yellow taxi cabs of New York.
I picture you in Watts, the 240-pound
  wrath of a bass player building up steam,
woodshedding for the strictly segregated
  hood, those who seek a tiny shot of God,
digging through hard pan, the hammer's
  grunt & blow. I need a gutbucket of gospel,
the flat land of cotton to catch all those

Chinese acrobats bubbling inside your head.
When I think of the day I will no longer
   hold a pencil within my hand or glance
upon the spines of my books, I hear
   Picasso's Guernica in your half-choked
cries, a gray workhorse lost in a fire's
   spiraling notes, a shrieking tenor sax
for the woman falling out of a burning house.
   I want to tell you if I wrote like you pick
& pat in *Blues and Roots*, I would understand
   the caravel of my childhood, loose
without oars or sails, rolling on the swells
   of a distant sea. That's all I got, Mr. Mingus.
I give you the archaeology of my words,
   every painstaking sound I utter when I come
to the end of a line, especially the stressed
   beats of a tiny country I lost long ago.

ERIKA AYÓN

Ashes

FOR SOUTH CENTRAL

As a child I walked down your sidewalks,
alleys, and streets. I thought you
were beautiful with your graffiti glittered
walls, the subtle sound of telephone poles
above us, the streets lined by palm trees.

The night in 1992, when you were set
on fire, I stood outside in the morning,
whispered prayers as I made crosses
with your ashes on my forehead.

Now, I notice your littered streets,
the letters on your walls no longer shine.
There are empty lots, boarded store fronts.
The sky seems to stay grey most days.

I want to litter your streets with poems.
To plant guerilla gardens of sunflowers
where the swap meets along
Vermont Avenue once stood.

I want to replace the shrines of those
that have been lost with shrines to you.
To shake you like a snow globe,
watch the ashes that remain fall.

When the moon is bright and full,
I'll decree silence, so everyone can hear
your heart beat, hear you exhale
the breath you have held for too long.

DANNY BAKER

Inalienable Right to Genuine Autonomy Nietzsche and Kierkegaard

I.

There's a wandering philistine in my bed,
looks lots like me but stoic & calm.
No sweat on the brow, just a little stress in
the translucent spine.
There's an inalienable right to misery, countenance
unfulfilling to many a farce,
      a wandering rhythm going off the charts but
        not for several weeks when airplays are tallied.
They can take yours, riding bareback to dilapidated
looping unhappiness in their misery.
Actually they can take mine first, but shall I choose,
not before I take it myself.

II.

Not before the peyote buzz & red rock consume
what I leave of myself.
Not before I let them know I meant business which is
no longer of concern to those policing mien.
Not before I bow at the altar of chronic antipathy,
lobbying inveterate blasphemy & what else is held dear
        for a dismantled whatever.
Before again, I admittedly talk to my reflection before
expectorating faces of death in boulders, a striking red.

III.

Before holding a séance to séances as nobody buys the
death rattle in the tall grass.
Before eating the last of the poison truffles left to pigs
which are equal but some more equal than others.
Before a lopsided world, never to be righted but in

imagination of dystopic moderation overpowering
        jungle rot gantries holding court on clay.
& the strong scent of fear from every corner, wafting
death in adulterated honesty chasing tail til the cows come home w/
        Johnny & a dirge for petitioned grins hiding
        hell under a crank case, long since banned by insincere
        artifice, repeating itself as it always repeats itself.
Before the Ravens have a ball from between the leftover leg
& final down hailing Mary in the fourth quarter.
Fear of god takes the charlatan by surprise, leading to a
hail of gunfire & god is dead.

ANDRES BERMEJO

Night, Sleep, Death, and the Stars

AFTER "A CLEAR MIDNIGHT" BY WALT WHITMAN

for those of us, who come in after a long
day of living, hoping, surviving without scars
family, friends, strangers all weaving

in night, reap sown seeds of day's dream
hastily hugging, holding a dimming
light, movements against all that seem
primordial, amoral, universal, screaming

in sleep, weeping bed bugs bite
betraying goodwill, rapid eyes moving,
spittle splattered pillows plight
wincing swaying truth's lullabies ring

in death, spirit wins when graves dug at ninety-one
while ending consumes consumers at their thriving
we seize, tear down walls crumbling for the young
neither age nor final rattle completely comforting

in the stars and faith we seek sameness
struggle with divinity's igniting,
infinite individuals to seek rest
from *a clear midnight* erupting

XOCHITL-JULISA BERMEJO

Ode to *Pan Dulce*

When I bathe you in the *aguas termales* of my coffee,
and you happily soak in the heat and steam,

what more can I do but place you on my tongue
and *recibirte como un* sacrament?

Your warmth radiates from my mouth
lighting the *esquinas oscuras* of my mind

where I find my *tata* planted on his corner stool
in the little pistachio kitchen in Boyle Heights.

Ojos brillantes, sugar dusting white stubble, he laughs.
Here his *sonrisa* grows and cancer never curls lips.

Panecito mio, lightweight and delicate in my palm,
periquito about to fly, I want to save you in tissue

like red chile picked from the yard already wrinkling.
Like unraveling yarn-end of dreams that tangle on wake

I throw myself into an embrace with a long dead friend.
I notice his favorite red jacket and think, *Where have you been?*

This is how you are *panecito*. A perfect holy circle
filling my hungry soul with lost loves that now and again *regresan*.

You are the warm silence that filled the air between
grandma *leyendo oraciones* and me reading poems.

You are *tata's* booming laugh. You are *el Español* swimming
in my mind. You are one single moment, a bite.

XOCHITL-JULISA BERMEJO

The Boys of Summer

CARPINTERIA, CA, JULY 2014

In Carpinteria, California a golden preteen in red shorts
runs down a clouded over beach to play at junior lifeguard.
He is lost in a sea of boys and girls just like him
all smiling and learning lessons on how to be safe.

In Brooks County, Texas, a boy with a note pinned to his shirt
addressed to an aunt in New Jersey wrestles
with his mother's hopes pinned to his shoulders.
Dehydration pins his cramping leg muscles together.

On a beach in Gaza four cousins play soccer.
One calls Messi while another calls Neymar before the injury.
The score is tied. They set up penalty kicks on the edge
of the surf. A boat in the distance sets up its shot.

The boy digs toes into sand and waits for his turn
to relay to a solo buoy bouncing in the water.
He asks the cute and sunny blond in line next to him,
"If you could live anywhere, where would you live?"

Alone in the desert, the boy lies down in the dirt.
As he closes his eyes he dreams of the home he is to build
for his mother and sister where he will watch all the T.V.
he wants, and no one worries about being killed.

On a beach in Gaza the four boys are blown to Jello-y pieces
of matter, and now they'll never know a life without fear.
The mothers and fathers gather outside the hospital and scream
into the air because they couldn't give their boys a safe place to play.

LAUREL ANN BOGEN
Blue Smoke and Steel

All nerve, this city
ferocious, it chews
and spits out
exhales blue
smoke and steel
and I am like this city
edging towards oblivion
the mirror cuts whatever facts
I have known about myself
woman/artist a quick fix
this identity a hook
to pin my nightclothes on
What do I know about reality?
celluloid captures my tinsel and frailties
as I jag through barrios and suburbs
mini malls pock the landscape

Los Angeles, *mi corazón*
what has become of you?

I remember fruit trees
blossoming like my dreams
of success now uprooted
by a concrete depression
we work
we wait
nothing comes
not synapse, sex, or sacrament

just the toil of the mundane
overblown by expectation
as it budges like a cancer
with no chance of remission

we go to bed at night
we get up in the morning
again and again and again

LAUREL ANN BOGEN

Hollywood Hills Noir

For Doug Knott

Aberration of weather studs
the sloe eyed city where change
gels in ripples after due process
I could go deeper
pry open the locked vault
below, combustible fossils bubble
in tar and petroleum beneath
Wilshire Blvd.—the jacaranda's roots
divide the house
Los Angeles
erupts in violet blossoms
each spring the profusion
is uncontained by stucco

Nature needs tending, of course
every few years the plates shift
the photogenic councilman is arrested
and somebody takes a fall
That's how I came here—by a calling
as surely as the devil herself
cloaked in the need to be seen
in filtered light
latticed with fault lines
and an underground whirlpool
as profligate as oil

F. DOUGLAS BROWN

What I Know about Watts

1.
>   comes from maps
> that when outlined is a kid

>   wearing a cap backwards head
> facing west to kiss the last bit of sun

>   but this is a distant relationship a drive-by
> with no bullets only two stick fingers

>   gesturing *deuces* or cut this
> cord—: *my past got me all caught up*

2.
>   comes from fiction rides me
> guilty for believing the narrative

>   folks live in fear   fear the iron
> gates on my eyes   fear the dark alley

>   I carve into my vision
> O trapped light & bleeding

>   ignorance   O fool for forgetting—:
> *yo' ass should know better*

3.
>   is really home Hunter's Point San Francisco
> hood sweet hood bliss & a boy

>   amongst the sets of dead brothers
> I have left: Shaheem & NayNay—

Danny Boy & Rick—
Ced & Tim where be your back talk

your dozens your mama jokes to
snap a nigga back to what made him

4.

should be my uncle Arbrit we'd roll Watts
all day—: concrete & graffiti & BBQ tinted windows

the black bull he was showed me how
to slap bones or drown a hornet's nest
both with gasoline he knew where
grandmama's favorite fried fish was this corn meal

crisp chore his Caddy his smile all should
be stuck at a four way stop in my brain—:

ain't no riot here man
ain't no riot here

F. DOUGLAS BROWN

Love Letter to Rashida Jones

AFTER MARCUS WICKER

dear dear Rashida I could spend
the next three days browsing

through images of just your hair
½ white ½ black strands of kindness:—

brunet streaks by day slang at night
but this would be mere fandom and what I need

is advice for my daughter who is all
cherry coke and a pack of bubble gum

all dust and chipped fingernails
I imagine she is you at twelve discretely claiming

all parts Peggy and Quincy:—caramel freckles
between a disarray of pre-teened brows

what my daughter knows of herself
she loves both the fight and funk found in her

unsettling curls she coils into a nest
of family stories made calm by water or tears

like your name she knows she can't hide
what makes her *I'm ethnic* you have said

to an industry that buys itself tan brushing away
both your white and black-ness she gets this

she gets your ease when correcting negligence
she gets that it could be a simple hand waving

across sand and stone   it can be as slight
as good manners   dearest Rashida like you her smile

could correct any ignorance but I know it
takes more than tricks and magic for a walnut

and honey-skinned girl whose half & half blood
swirls through my coffee dark skin and at times

away from it   will she wince when we talk
about lynchings or Tupac or Sandra Bland

will she know they were not accidents
or causalities of a quiet war   what is being waged

against her blood is as loud as genocide
my responsibility is not an empty basket

I'm only asking because she's close
to turning us off just to see your syndicated smile

glow from house to house   when she speaks
of you, she verifies your facts to hers

she dreams they are a dandelion away
I know this is supposed to be a love letter

and so I'll beg:—I need you Rashida
please tell her that black bodies are a blessing

like rain—:

like cinnamon—:

like Tupac and Sandra Bland

JEFFREY BRYANT

A Veteran's Day (2014)

Outside a store known and located
For its convenience
To customers near freeways and beaches
To vets near a hospital that can't hold them
At Wilshire and Barrington
He sits. His hat spells "Vietnam Veteran."
He asks for change,
Just a little,
Or a life's worth.
Whatever you can spare.

Vietnam is now a place travel show hosts visit,
Even John McCain.
John McCain does not ask anyone
For change.
Checks,
But not change.

He thanks me for what I give him.
I know his night will be long.
His sleep,
If he gets it,
Short, disrupted, worthless.
He has nothing to do tomorrow or the next day, but
This is not the freedom he fought for.

A breakfast awaits at a shelter.
The 720 will get him down there.
There, others with hats similar to his
Await,
Eat,
Talk,
Laugh,
Cry.

And then there was a Veterans Day
And I thanked him for his service
Like those who never served do
So they don't have to think about it for a while.
A picture pulled from his pocket revealed a friend
Whose laugh was suffocated by enemy fire,
Whose Marlboro tumbled from his lips, with blood to follow
Whose eyes opened wide enough to see life's slow fade
In the arms of the man I thanked.

How "thank you for your service" doesn't serve him at all.

I buy him coffee and as we part he calls me
Brother.
I now know what that means.
I am no longer an only child of the world.

RUTHIE BUELL
Artichokes

like lovemaking
the eating of artichokes
requires time.
the leaf,
like a tentative first kiss,
pulled between

gently but firmly

closed teeth

as the tiny emerald tip

caresses the tongue.
the mouth,

opening for more
and more
until only the
soft, gray undergarments remain,
these, eagerly

and skillfully removed,

leave only

the naked heart

to be shared,

seasoned
with buttery saliva and

ecstatically chewed and swallowed.
you cannot rush this act,
I know,
but sated in
the thistled afterglow
of an ancient assignation,
one cannot help but wonder,
who were the first in the tribe,

the first to stay

behind in the cave,
the first to initiate

this culinary cunnilingus,

while others remained

in the field,
consuming

from their kill,
the still warm

and bloody liver,
with a Paleolithic

Yum.

DON KINGFISHER CAMPBELL

Ventura Highway

Dude walks Los Feliz Blvd. into Glendale
Neon signs making cool the darkness
In his unsurprising dark blue windbreaker
He sits by his bearded self in Del Taco
After buying a $1.49 special burrito
With a dollar bill, one quarter, two dimes
And a smile (did I fail to mention one bandaged finger?)
He looks around for anyone looking
Then pulls out of his nylon gym bag
A bottle of beer, takes a few hearty swigs
To wash down that cheap El Scorchio sauce
He twists back the twist-off
Disgusted, slides around out of his seat
And staggers across the corporate honeycomb carpet
While a song by America plays

LUÍS CAMPOS

Andrés

The phone rings… it's Mitch,
Andrés is dead from bullet wounds
after being held up in his taxi…

Sunday, in Whittier,
we gather at the Jewish funeral parlor…
at the pulpit, a man who had never met Andrés
recites a pre-packaged eulogy…

The roses I brought fall next to the coffin,
traditional small loose rocks
are on many of the tombstones—
tears slide closer to the dirt…

Back to the Santa Ana Freeway…
in Hollywood we meet at Tony Torres'
for a noisy, stoned farewell
to the tune of Puerto Rican bongos and rum…

The black taxi driver gets drunk,
David and I play chess…

Large tokes & small conversation.

JESSICA M. WILSON CARDENAS
Being Human

feeling desolate
in this space
where time meshes into the host of my debt.
uncertain slumber of rite; a net of collection.

why does it always come down to money;
to raise your hope
your praises
to make you feel like a good human,
a happy human?

justify me this feeling of incompleteness
because i don't have enough paper
to go around
taking away all the hands i owe.

is my life less valuable
because i cannot pay someone today?
is my life less valuable
since i don't have enough green to pay?

am i demeaned to sidewalk skids
and tire tread because I came up short?

how short of human am i since i have no green to give?
since when did paper interject itself into veins?
do needles blend it into the stream
of blood
plasma
capillaries
dust?

there is no green in my blood.
i am not rich.
i am not paper.
i'm human.

ANAID CARRENO
Snake Tongue: *Lengua de Culebra*

Permission to speak, I am the ally of the silenced and unheard.

I am the noise you can't shake.

Two sharp points like the accents I carry on my tongue.

I slither and squirm as I observe what they have done to you.

It's a tragedy what they think of you and how arrogantly they use you for self-proclaimed prophecies.

No! I am not that! I yell loudly, but only the echo replies.

Incarceration, deportation, degradation, gentrification some of the words that burn as I spit them out.

False ideologies are accepted as realities ignoring the facts.

I am not illegal and you don't have the right to label or decide.

I am not a criminal, never was.

Don't obstruct my academic path, I will jump each and every obstacle one by one.

I was born free, you labeled and shackled me with lies and hatred but I broke loose.

With my forked tongue I battle your double-sided knife.

I am not content with the destructive pattern that has emerged with your avarice.

I will not kill for you and I will not die in vain.

My snake-like tongue has no mercy and will not cease until I see dignity and peace.

ILIANA CARTER

Mygration

Texistepeque. The countryside. El Salvador, 1930.
rivers and stones, toucans and trees, flowers of fire, tortillas and black beans,
days of cutting coffee, cutting cotton, cutting your hands,
fighting with the boss, making *tamales* and *pupusas* to sell without being
able to eat,
my dear grandmother,
i know it hurt you to have nothing but cardboard houses for your children,
but cardboard or not, how much more it hurt you to have them ripped
from your hands,
strong, working hands,
hands that gave the rich so much to eat,
hands that could no longer cradle your babies.

a woman scorned, brutalized,
the fire that must have burned in her,
courage forged into black diamonds,
beat into shape by his violence
she fled with those dark stars inside her.

a little moon waited for her
alone in her room,
doors made of tin,
cotton sheets used as makeshift walls.

San Salvador, 1960.
a city so small.
a 5-year-old girl slept in a bed with four others
without a mother, looking for a way out.
always seeking to move forward,
typing classes, English classes, nights at the Japanese factory,
days before the Washington bullets began,
when her friends began disappearing in the night,
when she had to burn her pictures of Che,
she left.

21 years old,
crossing three borders,
cracked yellow desert,
deep black river,
thorns, dirt, blood,
crossing through hell to seek her heaven,
arriving at last, in the city of angels.

heaven, it was not.
Los Angeles, 1980.
years had passed in the grinding of factories,
raising children who were not hers,
cutting paper, cutting straws, cutting fabric with machines,
days cut short without her brothers, without friends, without family,
she met a blue-eyed man,
a tall man, with light hair,
and she cut her last name.

her daughter was born with brown skin and orange hair.
Cafe con leche, she would tell me,
coffee from my mother, cream from my father.

Echo Park, 1984.
i played in an apartment with many helicopter moons,
homeboys blasting,
white lines on the table,
neighbors with tats 'n' guns,
Scarface on Christmas day,
the *veterano* on the corner who liked to steal my brother's ice cream,
el vato loco who was known for taking ears and noses if you pissed him off,
my neighborhood, with its palm trees, its burning sun,
my hair burned orange and red just like Sunset Boulevard,
dandelions on the concrete,
my beautiful city.

they took us from there.
running from bullets once again.
they didn't leave one civil war to find another.
we left, fleeing to the north once more.

San Francisco. Oakland, Berkeley. 1990.
my heart, my grandmother took me by the hand everywhere,
now without the familiar streets of Sunset, no Alvarado,
abuelita, with hands like mine, walked me through my life,
those hands that could finally caress the tiny face of her child,
those hands that held me as she died and called me *hija*, her very own
daughter,

my dear grandmother's hands prayed for me every night
in the fog of the Bay, whispered nighttime prayers until i left
seeking the same stars my mother did.

Westwood, Los Angeles, 2000.
grey apartments, no color, no humor, no music, no children,
white studies.
i missed you so much, mother, grandmother,
when i realized it wasn't stars i was seeking, but the sun within you.

Echo Park, Boyle Heights, East LA, Pico Rivera, Baldwin Park, Fontana,
2003, 2010, 2015.
my family, my veins.
my music, my *cumbia,*
norteños, mariachis,
enchiladas y cafe con leche,
punk rock children and neighbors singing as they clean,
Morrissey, the Smiths, my Rockabilly queens,
everyone's Chente,
trumpets, parties on the weekend,
kids crying and laughter everywhere,
drama on the streets,
the beautiful heat of the sun like your hands,
my love,
my sun,
my moon,
my everything,
just like you two.

and that's why i belong here.
First and Soto.
my life on the gold line.
gold.
Just like your love.

gold.
the stars we sought were within us.

JESSICA CEBALLOS
two dreams

I can finally remember the two dreams I had last night.

The last one.
Three large brown eggs
blemished, broken and half-cooked yolk running from the uneven cracks.
I cooked them, ate them.

Everything will be ok.

*

The first one.
I watched myself walking out of a hotel room in San Francisco, walking down a long and forever-spiraling road. Me, an octogenarian Japanese American woman, and her Mexican American great-granddaughter. In a blink the road led to an oily rainbow-colored cavernous tunnel that funneled into a wide-open but blackened ocean. I remember thinking it was man-made. A beautiful Earth catastrophe, man-made.

We were looking at the walls together, trying to remember if this is where we were supposed to be. The stucco-like sand colored exteriors under the thin skin the oil painted of itself is not supposed to be this beautiful. When layered on thin, you forget the oil and the damage done. But we could just as easily see what was, what is, and what will be, through this mess we always make of this place we both live in. It's not supposed to be this easy, or this beautiful.

I told her and her great-granddaughter that I wanted to take photos of this place, to remember what it feels like, when times were worse and better. There was something beautiful about the crevasses between two stalagmites reaching for the open air, and the glistening black oil that made its way in and through those crevasses. Almost like watching the sun chisel time onto our skin, in slow motion.

I don't think she wanted me to take those photos. And I don't know if I did. But when I woke up I realized that she had already lived through the messes of our years. She was telling me something, carrying the message and our dreams by the hand.

Though I saw them rotting, blemished and half-cooked, somehow she managed to break them open, rendering the raw yolks tempting enough to eat. Tempting enough for me to see, taste, and to dream of the open air, our skin, and the oil we cover it in.
To uncover it.

Everything will be ok.

JESSICA CEBALLOS

Joaquín lives in Los Ángeles

A LETTER DEDICATED TO "CORKY" GONZALES. EMBEDDED IN THIS POEM
ARE EXCERPTS OF HIS MONUMENTAL, AND STILL RELEVANT, 1967 POEM
"I AM JOAQUIN" AS SETTING.

"Yo Soy Joaquín,
lost in a world of confusion,
caught up in the whirl of a gringo society,
confused by the rules, scorned by attitudes,
suppressed by manipulation, and destroyed by modern society." *1967*

It was the roaring cauldron of the Angeles.
What became of the Battle of Chavez Ravine, but still
sports enthusiasts frolicked in the Elysian sun.
'65 Watts Riots, and war—
what were they good for?
But at least the dancing *huera* became Whiskey A Go Go.
God bless Sunset Boulevard, after all.
In '66 *They* allowed us to learn what it means to be Mexican-American.
I said, in '66 they *allowed* us to validate our history.
At San Fernando Valley College, in 1966,
Los Angeles is free to learn about us, Mexican-Americans.
Fast forward, very forward. The progress of March '68
They became threatened by us living as Mexican-Americans,
learning as Mexican-Americans, so
Wilson, Lincoln, Roosevelt, and Garfield showed them Chicano.
March of '68.

and the fight continued   and continued   and continues,
until the river runs dry. And fatigue washes the brown off our skin.

"My land is lost and stolen, My culture has been raped. I lengthen the line at
the welfare door and fill the jails with crime. These then are the rewards this
society has for sons of chiefs and kings And bloody revolutionists who gave a
foreign people all their skills and ingenuity" *1967*

Our present, ignored.
Our history that once shouted, now only barely a whisper on our streets,

62

our walls, in our homes, and backyards.
Dis-placed, re-moved, and re-defined to special programs, on special days.
A cultural dismay, becoming an intellectual opportunity.
The Arroyo Seco *no esta seco* any more.
And the L.A. River has survived this drought.
El Movimiento

esta moviendo.

"A foreign people…"

"…Changed our language and plagiarized our deeds as feats of valor of their
own. They frowned upon our way of life and took what they could use. Our
art, our literature, our music, they ignored—so they left the real things of
value and grabbed at their own destruction by their greed and avarice." *1967*

Our arte, *Our* literatura, *Our* musica
is not for sale on Olvera Street, or Grand Park,

"*La Raza!*
Méjicano!
Español!
Latino!
Chicano!
Or whatever I call myself, I look the same I feel the same I cry and
Sing the same.
I am the masses of my people and I refuse to be absorbed. I am Joaquín.
The odds are great But my spirit is strong,
My faith unbreakable,
My blood is pure.
I am Aztec prince and Christian Christ.
I SHALL ENDURE!
I WILL ENDURE!"

ADRIAN ERNESTO CEPEDA

Traffic buzzing a familiar refrain

All exhaust, breathing confused
fuming with my flashing signal
annoyance turned up to eleven
same old gridlock song
seeing the closed ramp sign—
why is it too late to change lanes?
Last minute, no exit, no movement
no rubber burning, feel me
honking proudly hear me vent.
Just another morning drive,
fast lane stalled;
window cracks, sweat while breaking
my other foot longs to push
down pedal, steering, antenna
scrambles KCRW spinning
static-ing loudly mouthing words
from David Byrne's lost Talking
Heads lament; on this road Kerouac
never could imagine, raging nowhere
just another summer stranded
on this anticlimactic highway
as combustible temper rises
still fuming
while these signals keep flashing
my L.A. discontent.

ADRIAN ERNESTO CEPEDA

Her moon over Los Angeles

FROM THE PHOTOGRAPH ISTANTANEA BY HELMUT NEWTON

I love the way she leans
against the balcony
teasing over Sunset
Boulevard, Chateau Marmont
showing off her beautifully round
skin, ready for me to honor her
cheekiest glow; before my telescope
lens angles her close up behind,
so well defined even astronomers
at Griffith Park Observatory
would be pointing their eyes
past Hollywood signs,
as her sunset strips
and traffic down below
would try adjusting their mirrors
already knowing
I have the most perfect rearview
shining in heels so eloquently
in our City of Angels; I wish
you could feel, from the balcony
as exhaust perfumes, how palm
trees bow their heads to this beauty,
as her fullest moon spreads
softly for me.

ANGEL CERRITOS
La Calaca

She walked
in a white gown
Neither spiteful nor
angry

She walked

Chains clanked
against the wheels
of her cart

And they knew
she was on her way

The moon bit into the sky,
making it bleed
a million stars

The old man cried,
"María!"
"No," she replied

Her hand
like a *calaca*
against his bony shoulder

Cold and deaf
the old man lay

The candlelight gone
with a sigh from the
Night

She walked
in a white gown
metal clanking against
the wheels of her cart

And they knew,
She would be back
for someone else

ROBERT CHAMBERS

Poem for Lost Angels

It was where the seasons changed.
Before my visions were lost in the L.A. sun,
and the hard light of reality had put the
weight onto my feet. It was where
the lush green Oaks, and Maples,
and Cottonwoods, Black Walnuts, all shed
their leaves, and multicolored rainbows swirled
to fall upon the canopy, a carpet laid out for a King,
like rose petals strewn across our bed.

And the winds, soft and cool, and scented
in the Cedar's perfume, caressed at the cheeks
so painless, yet devoid of winters bite
in autumn, in late afternoon, but to rise up in fury
across the Kansas plain, across the icing rivers in
evening with the turning of the celestial spheres
and the arrival of the moon.

It is this. I remember now with my child's eyes,
the wind, and that if I ran fast enough, fast as I
could, and caught it at a certain angle at my back,
I could fly with the Angels.

LISA CHEBY

Guests in a Guileless Land

Aloe Vera wanes to pink to match its pot—
no more native here than the green grass
that thrives on sprinklers of life support,

or palms that wave their fans—a gesture
to guard the homes that hug the hilltops.
The birds tweet their protest and the tires orate
"one-O-one" against the asphalt.

From the balcony below, we get wind
of jasmine smothered by cigarette smoke.
Or is it gardenia's white whiff? I cannot see

over the rail, cannot see this desert whose dust
adorns our armchairs, armoires, and cedar-lined trunks.

LISA CHEBY

When a Sonnet Loses Track of the Seasons

For months I wait for winter to return
to wrap his ice slate silk around my own
mourning. Rather, he sends me heat that spurns
surrender: who could sleep in his browned
valley? No rest, the holidays burn
forward. All I saved is useless now:
boots, sweaters, duvets, love. I yearn,
but must relent: winter forgot this town.

Surprised that I lost a whole season?
In spring, an entire plane disappeared
in a sea. Just gone, without a reason,
no black box to explain, to give easing
to this thirst for other than what you feared:
this absence, this act of treason.

GABREAL CHO

Breast

Women scrub backs
as if to wash away sins of property.
Hair streams
and coats appendages.
Female of hair and
ditto copy stand side by side,
with hands centered toward mid-body.
They gently rub clean folds that mark them
the other half.
I see one in haste
to make herself clean.
Chest meets lap to hide an eye that winks.
Though this face I've yet to meet,
it speaks, and I blink.

CHIWAN CHOI

if 100, then 150

EXCERPTS FROM A WORK IN PROGRESS

the floor
is invisible under suitcases and boxes

we are in the process of beginning again
purging

boxing up regrets
and shipping them to a new home

we've been at this for days
i can't even remember

the things
now hidden

that we are saving

*

there is an image in my head
of me lying on my back
on the ground outside the world trade center

it was 1989
and gary had told us to do that and look up
he said the building would look like it was going to fall on me

i remember visualizing it as he spoke
i remember lying there on the ground

but i can't ever remember
what it is that i saw
what it was that took my breath away

*

there was another time
i saw him on the street

i noticed his slumping left shoulder
first
then the rest of him
like the face that couldn't smile

i asked dad where he was going

he could only say that it was for a walk

there was nothing more to ask

so i let him pass
my hand briefly on his back

unable to watch him go

*

it has been days
three or four

since i thought of him

i have been sitting on the porch
watching the unfamiliar rain
asking over and over again:
where is this light born?

days away from 45
trying to leave myself in fragments
on pavement walked on
by strangers that could never care

because this is how i will find peace

and that moment of remembering well
how he sat on the couch
his teeth pulled out for the night
and turned to speak to me

MARCUS CLAYTON

Schizophrenic on the Steps of Bank of America

In maroon silk, she talked to the wind
animated to the point
of her designer bracelets
clanking like rusted pans,
chatting over the clatter
of her necklace—pearls bleached
hung loose
from her chocolate
neck—staring into an empty
parking structure, holding
its eye contact
more than the eyes of the mother
draped with oversized cotton,
hand clung to a jaunty child
who shoved dollars into the maroon
woman's flailing fingers.
She broke her convulsions
grinned for the child
and let ants climb
polyester around her legs
when the mother scurried
in achromatic Nikes
washed with dirt.

ANDA COLEMAN

Sonnet for Austin

AFTER A LINE BY E. ETHELBERT MILLER

I love you as the grass loves the stone

I do not love you as if you were salt-pork or opal
or the sorrow of grass widows tending fields.
I love you as uncertain fingers foil tenderness
in public, where all eyes witness our coverings.

I love you as the wind loves the tumbleweed
and carries it across the sand to its lair of secrets.
I love you as chocolate loves cinnamon risen
from my breath to revive the poem in your eyes.

I love you as today loves yesterday—the way Billie loved Prez.

RAFA CRUZ

My Mind on the 239

The kind of beautiful that makes you dream.
The clues are mystical, you're deep beneath,
A smoky, spiritual, entrancing stream,
Of pink, subliminal, honey sweets.

I might not be critical when I speak,
But my judgment's a hole in a heart that beats.
My love is cynical, don't believe,
My words; they're cyclical broken dreams.

I'm a sinister ritual, a wondrous storm,
A loving, habitual man of the poor.
Not known by many, by many adored.
I've given you plenty, you're asking for more.

ILIANA CUELLAR

Canto In Two Lenguas

My lips quiver trying to mimic the shape of my grandmother's.
Form my tongue to roll with the vibrations of...
que raro es cambiar de Inglés to Spanish...
Mispronouncing my name so it's easier to digest,
so my white teachers can easily call roll.
Why must we bite one tongue to let the other speak
split expressions into my assimilated half?
I think translated making sense to myself and
when I read, I read *Español* in English.
I wish I could dream in Ch's and Rr's to speak to my
grandparents about the *milpa* and times before the dollar.
What could a single *colón* buy you and why does everything
I buy with U.S. money taste so bitter?
The *platanos* I savor in the morning don't taste as sweet as
the mangoes Papa Chendo picked.
The *pupusas* are bigger but not as tangy
and the diaspora's yells resonate louder on the other side.
I pretend I can't hear them like my grandmother
pretends she can hear me over the phone.
She's losing her hearing but the calling card only allows so many
minutes for us to speak in broken sentences to match our hearts.

YAGO S. CURA
Los Angeles County Jail Sonnets, #5

It gets difficult to distinguish between Tuesday and Wednesday
between heat, hot water, 3 squares and a Spa Lobotomy, between
not brushing your teeth and not wiping your ass, between a copy-machine lien
and having a class set of books to read aloud as part of your reading regiment.

It gets hard to say whether trustees are house slaves or snitch-custodians;
if waiting for pill call to commence programming amuses the nurses,
or makes them prickly, apple-bottom cacti; if the food that is disbursed
in the Officer's Dining Room is served legitimately, or as closed-circuit joke.

Jail is the real Mother of Invention: I have seen shoelaces made from the elastic
of a T-shirt, I have seen three miniscule toothbrushes lashed together to form
a wavelet-taming brush, I have seen a playing card used as a telescope,
        a rhinoplasty
performed with golf pencils, and portraits of 2 Pac, Mandela, and Rosa Parks
made entirely from Bologna. I have seen Pruno percolated from Scariyaki,

I have seen youth lose their mind, convicted by hearsay, double-crossed
        by crimeys.

YAGO S. CURA
Watts Shadormas, #1

"Willowbrook"
Green, Imperial
Section Eight,
Plaza Mex.,
busy-bee Long Beach Bull-yard.
Fueling, fixing, please.

One oh five,
east 80 miles per
stitch in time
'65
east of pass. or west of pass.,
big invisible.

Reverend
Pike's candid report
card, effort-
lessly tells
Yorty, Parker they're hiding
delicate praytells.

Frye Brothers,
catalyst-riding
Armyman
little 'bro
two blocks from Ma's casa
come out in rollers.

Public homes,
courtyard laundrylines,
fuzzy all-
eys and lots,
Crips, Bloods, mafia spinsters,
grizzly mattresses.

ART CURRIM

It Is Upon Us

TO THE WORLD'S MIGRANT WORKERS
AND THEIR FRACTURED FAMILIES

It is upon us, then
The sun casts long shadows in its lazy retreat
Made hazy by standing dust
A king without a kingdom passes his dream
To a prince without a homeland
This is all I have
Says the aging monarch
His regal voice heavy
This is all I could protect for you
It is wrapped in parchment
The cord that binds it is from my inauguration gown
It is blown in sand
Damp from the sweat of honest labor
Dried against these cheeks withered
when i had no tears left to shed
Do not ever unwrap this, it is your dream
The dream you will one day pass to your child
That they may try to escape their long shadow
Reconcile to their purpose
To their destiny
Guard it with your life
Hold it dear with love
You must know what to do
When you are called upon to use it

KAMAU DAÁOOD

Los Angeles

the angels here
have pigeon's wings
blue collars
washed in sweat
the common salt
in tears
tongues swirl
in a stew of cultures
singing asphalt songs
in the mist of seagulls
bebop atop
the San Andreas
a humble plate
of beings

DOREN DAMICO
Unfurl My Spirit

Above all things
I have sold
Given away
Left rotting
Or cast off
I let go
Unfurl my spirit

Above all things
I have learned
Puzzled over
Slowly devoured
Rightly discerned
I now know
Unfurl my spirit

Above all things
I have become
A Jackie-in-the-Box
Who pops out
Springs away
I am all
Unfurl my spirit

Above all things
I have seen
The essential
Life struggle
Unto death
I laugh low
Unfurl my spirit

Above all things
I left behind
From dark earth
Into light
My tattered body
Crumbling below
Unfurl my spirit

Woman of Colors

I am a woman of colors
You try to white me out
As if I am merely emptiness
Clumsy surface consciousness
Like salty seeds, I spit you out
Laughing at your foolishness

My barefoot black
Calloused soles
My lengthy limbs
Brown fringed
I have walked the paths
Of our aboriginal daughters'
Unknown destiny

My courses red
Blood of life
Seeping pink
Luscious lips
I have run the islands
Of our aboriginal sisters'
Righteous fury

My curving hips
Forest green
Rainbow spring
Indigo youth
I have danced the steps
Of our aboriginal witches'
Mountain ecstasy

My ample breasts
Dark tipped

Milky crests
Blue waves
I have sailed the oceans
Of our aboriginal mothers'
Courageous journey

My flowing hair
Blonde child
Auburn woman
Silver crone
I have seen the depths
Of our aboriginal grandmothers'
Wisdom mystery

My sienna skin
Hazel eyes
Salty tears
Yellowed teeth
I have sung the song
Of our aboriginal Goddesses
Chewing Herstory

I am a woman of colors
You try to white me out
As if I am merely emptiness
Clumsy surface consciousness
Like salty seeds, I spit you out
Laughing at your foolishness

CAROL V. DAVIS

Driving Late at Night in Hollywood with a Foreign Visitor

Past the neon signs raw as splinters.
The kid stumbling down the sidewalk
as if unaccustomed to the confinement of shoes.
The tourists taking turns like chess pieces,
snapping photos in front of Grauman's Chinese Theater
to admire back home, settling into a crowded booth
for tea and steamed dumplings.
Past the tattoo parlor that offers more than decoration.
My visitor has never been so tempted.
Movie star maps for sale, smiling posters of all his idols.
Don't get me wrong.
I know we should make a place for Elvis,
but the cracked Naugahyde in the diner is a body falling apart,
the oozing stuffing cries out for stitches.
More than the televangelist can deliver.
He's talking to my visitor.
If only he'd fork over the hard-earned dollars
he'd saved for this vacation.
Go have a drink in Hooters.
The busty waitresses are only college students
trying to earn book money.
Why not appreciate what's God given?
It's getting late, time to drop off my visitor.
He'll unpack, lay the striped shirts his wife
so carefully folded in the long drawer,
pick up the Bible from the nightstand.
It doesn't matter that he can barely speak the language.
There's salvation there.
He only needs to decipher the alphabet.

IRIS DE ANDA

terra firma

unwinding inside these bones
a pulse of rushing waters
melted invocations
flowing in a river of sun
close eyelids
memory tumbles
down into remembrance
tree bark on the shore of shallow depths
dry creeks of dusted dreamers
intertwine with wet mud on skin
peel away layers of lost
pray silently over the edge of boulders
stand in silhouette of midnight
unmask the rolling thunder in your song
strike land of your ancestors
with lightning in your breasts
shine twilight from your tongue
as violets and vultures serenade
forgotten stories
uncover coyote medicine
trickster of trust
teller of tales
come home
to sacred valley
of red hawk and elephant hills
singing praises to the spirit
of river which once flowed along this land
give thanks and kiss cracked cement
moist lips deposit seeds of sea
into abyss that is our barren world
until the ceremony of our breath
conjures enough tears
to water our next steps

SEVEN DHAR

When I Smoked Pencils

It started at night
when I would write
ill until
my instrument would alight
and alight
and smoke—
brought it up to my mouth,
inhaled,
I toked,
tickled by the taste of lead,
the unadulterated *shhh*,
No. 2,
unfiltered,
short bus color coated,
sweet chicory cudgel,
charred chopstick—
light, airy balsa,
cedar, unscented,
juniper, amalgamated
particle pulp,
the better the sharpening,
the shaving,
splintered shards
splaying,
nervous impressions,
incisive vampire marks
stabbing, sucking
my areola's,
my bronchioles,
the nipples
slicing through my chest—
an ecstasy of contractions,
a shiver of the esophagus

ill until
I coughed
blackened flecks,
squiggles—
little corrections in red:
the last thing I wrote
when I smoked
pencils.

DAVID M. DIAZ

an addiction

When the clouds finally soak
into the mountain,
let the sun burn shadows
onto clean concrete
Angeleno heir-
loom tomatoes, only organic will do;
only un-afflicted chickens
for my eggs please—
while I fill my lungs with fake
sage vapor.

Bended boroughs connected
by 469 miles of broken freeway:
carpool tendrils spit oil and dust
into the ocean   a body vexed
and charmed with the attention.

I can't leave.
I tip toe around the umbilical
cordially invited to the park
where man sleeps and watches
suited man work just as hard
at something else   On the subway:
not allowed to eat your sandwich
but please,
youngster,
let me have two
snickers and some cigarettes instead.
The train blurs past charred and vacant
squatters' mansions, pushing past
the crest of t.v. antennas, wobbling
to a stop for us to see the rocky backdrop
and ogle what Castro handed Fremont
in a fit of haste.

Baby-blue specked
with palm and yellow hue.
Breathing is supposed to hurt like this,
injured for reminiscence.
I always love the flush of city framed
in brilliant lights, all at once
through the window of a descending
airplane so I forever admire her lost patina.
Standing on a Sunday street
in downtown   heart in beat with the sirens
shrieked up soap washed windows
before their echoes break the sky.

My tether's only loosely fit;
my ankle keeps a crooked gaze to hold it warmly.

KIM DOWER

Fontanel

He's so lucky
the brain doctors
tell me, huddled in white
their names embroidered

in blue script across
their chests, my grown son
sprawled across the hospital bed
tubes, needles sticking

into his body, twined
around him like veins
through a parched leaf.
I can't look at him

his mouth crusted
unfocused eyes
that yesterday lit up
the room, now his skull

fractured, same head
I used to hold in one hand
his legs rocking my arm
to sleep. Infant's heads

are so soft, easy
to rupture, brains still
forming. I can't look at him now
his giant hands, filth baked

under his nails
from scratching the gutter
where he fell off
the back of a car—

of course he shouldn't have
been sitting on the trunk
of a car—but you see
they will do things

they will do things
that can hurt and we have to watch
and when I see him in that bed
hooked up to machines beeping

instructions to the nurse
making noise like garbage trucks
on collection day
I have to look away

cover my eyes like he did
when he was three
afraid to see
the flying monkeys

in the *Wizard of Oz*,
he'd run screaming
into my lap. Where is it now
The Emerald City?

Where can I get the courage
to uncover my eyes
see the blood
ooze from his ear

walk over to the bed
whisper, *I'm here, it'll be ok*
you're lucky, the doctors say
but all I can think

is what if it hadn't
gone this way—
luck, the slippery slope
of miracles, unpredictable

fragile as a fontanel
soft luck running out
from the moment
we're born.

KIM DOWER

Workout

I crunch my stomach

as the gym televisions blast:

interview about "Bra Balls"

women demonstrating

how you can wash your bras

worry free three at a time

keeps dainty delicates

from being crushed, twisted

even different colors won't bleed

on the other channel local woman

gets shot waiting for bus

no time to worry about *her* bras

worry like hunger lasts forever

I don't wear a bra close my eyes

turn up my I-Pod let the tunes

drench my eardrums drown out

sounds I never asked to hear

hands clasped behind my head

lift to the beat again again press

my lower back tight against the mat

stomach clenched jaw angry can't stop

thinking of the woman bleeding

on the curb even bra balls

seem more real noise blasting

gunfire for the workout lift again

again while someone else's stomach

is emptying into the gutter

SHARIF DUMANI
Los Angeles

Transient inflammation.
Swollen to the point of nearly bursting.
Since birth, and most likely till death, will we hold hands across decaying memories of structures that have risen and fallen, areas that have been long since gone under the grip of development.
An "out with the old, in with the new" policy that leaves an ocean full of lost, lonely and displaced.
Solace is on mountaintops or alleyways.
Sex can be found everywhere, but comfort is a luxury that only the privileged or enlightened can afford.
With the cold chill of opportunity, the prospects of wealth or fame brightly flash on every streetlight, but compassion lies in food trucks and soup kitchens between 3rd and 7th.
It's the heart and soul.
As grown children set up playgrounds across soon-to-be neighborhood graveyards, barrios and "wastelands" become ripe for the picking.
Gardens built by momma's own hands, now bought and sold, somehow lose that gentle touch.
Food for the soul, now food to be sold at a price no one can afford.
Yet through all of this, there has never been more love bubbling beneath the surface, poking out through every crack in the sidewalk, or kind smile.
It's unstoppable, and ultimately, unbreakable.
Like chains built to guard and seal in, the key to lock or unlock lies in its people.
A community of dreamers, believers, and failure survivors, sewn into the fabric of the city, keep it from wear and tear and lack of care.
To finally understand, that the only love that's ever needed, is the love of the ground on which you stand.

SHARIF DUMANI

I Went and Saw You Again, Tonight

I went and saw you again tonight. That peach hair glowing against a stage-lit backdrop of white, violet, yellow, and blue. I trick myself every time, thinking that I can handle it, but it just gets rawer, to the point where the slightest touch of memory brings an excruciating jolt. As I stood there, in my cubbyhole in the dark, I felt a sense of embarrassment, embarrassment for myself. How I could still be trapped underneath your fingertips without you putting the slightest pressure. Have mercy! The power you unknowingly possess is as great as a power set out to destroy. Like shards of shrapnel from an explosion, you can run away five hundred feet and still feel the slice. Clueless, bobbing your head from side to side to soaring sweeps and cascading lines, I stared straight into your eyes. You couldn't see me. To tell you the truth, it wouldn't matter if you had. I walked out. My past was on fire that night. The same raging heat as the night we burned in flames on Glendale Blvd. Third degree love. There's no insurance on romance. Our house burned down and I have yet to find a home. You, unscathed, radiant, as if the flames illuminated every movement while I hung on to anticipation to see how each could be more beautiful than the next. Fuck my life. L.A. took me down. That's what I heard, that's what I saw, and ultimately that's what it did.

CHRISTIAN ELDER

Queer

here
the rain is having phone sex
on a murdered cordless
with my gray hands
beating relentless taps
over the dial-tone
and i have drunk 7 bottles
of bladder
that kept me up at night
and told me to
my heart is a basehead
that pumps my nerves full of powder
until my cheeks flake off
into the wings that broke
supper with the john

the hemp is walking
down an aisle
of a small neighborhood
in the last supermarket of
size d cups
hermetically sealed

at 5:05 am
some of the laymen are
curt with me
through the hazy storefront
of a low-budget movie still
because they'd rather be
stage actors

hollywood
in its wet lime-colored skin

pines away
as every adult bookstore on the strip
looks like a bad toupee
and even i
with my roach clip know
that the power to stare
agrees with any wretched dreamscape
whenever i wear my floral chaps
like a square inch of meat
in the rain

SETH ELPENOR
From California…

This land is our land.

Our orange fields beneath the new blue sky
The blue not as it was but as it has come to be
The new blue crafted by you and me.

Our complexes of trailers and avant-garde architecture
Sprawled out at the feet of mountains.
Staking our claim.

Our roads beaten into the dirt
By walking wanderers and driven wheels,
Cemented into the earth with tar.

This land is our land;

We will do with it what we wish,
And we wish to tackle it
Conquer it with our culture
Tame the woman whose tit we suck
Claw at her back and bite at her flesh
Show her we are here to stay.

She will not fight.
She will wait.
She is closer to eternity than our proudest monument,
And when the last of us are gone,
Her oceans shall shatter our piers;
Her creatures shall strip away our homes;
Her fields shall tear away the tar.
And in time her scars shall fade.

This land was made for you and me.

FRANCISCO ESCAMILLA (BUS STOP PROPHET)

Graf-ight

he said he wants to be Dali, Rivera, Kahlo
and that the sharpie in his hand makes it so
the seats on the bus canvases awaiting creation
every window an ancient pyramid wall
calling for his story to be told
etched in within seconds
with a precision that brings about questions of extra terrestrial meaning
makes him immortal
invokes portals into areas of his imagination
that public school recreation could never tap
so he taps tips with his fingerprints to convince himself he does more than
    just exist
scratches truth into used textbooks to feel something
plays his love supreme on freeway overpasses
with cans spitting soul notes
in colors that make people wish they could listen with their eyes
his hands cry purpose
breathe fire
exhale dreams in passionate moans of release
a taste of freedom
an act of defiance that frees him

he said he wants to be Guevara, Chavez, Menchu
and that the stencil in his hand makes it so
arm raised
hand clenched into a fist wrapped around his revolution
he sprays a mist that causes children's thoughts to spiral
ideas of an art undying
still present
still presents an image of peaceful resolutions
no matter how many times society tries to coat it
with explicit layers of vandalism
with a flick of his fingers he flares foresight

of rising like the sun at the height of its glistening
he's listening
paying attention
provoking intention from those who can't afford not to look
speaking a language that their souls remember
that their marrow recognizes as their own
where echoes of once upon a times seep into stone

he said he wants to be somebody, anybody, more than just a body in a
    head count
and the movement in his hands makes it so
he doesn't understand why it's a crime to wake up walls from their
    dormant state
why he has to run like bad paint
from reds and blues who see the world in black and white

he wants to create windows on barriers so people can see each other
so he can be seen
the separation makes him sick

make his cans cough colors in clumps
causing his creativity to thicken around his throat
obstructing his breath
until he can't say anything anymore

Boyle Heights

East of the Angeles river is all I ever knew of Eden
Where maize mingles in mariachi dreams
Aztlan murals stain the eyes of the working class
Where immigrant footprints proud and exhausted
Bleed the stories of our peoples' past.

Boyle Heights is a culture on fire
A pair of shoes dangling from telephone wire
Dancing to salsa music in the sky
A five star backyard restaurant
Composing miracles into mole recipes
Magic into Menudo on a Sunday morning
Soothing the sounds of an all too familiar hungers cry

Boyle Heights is street corner rosaries for fallen flowers
Candles burning faithful for hours
Chalk line souls lying silent on the street
In the wake of *pachuco* whispers
Rising like sidewalk vapors
Tortured by the summer heat

Boyle Heights is a language of legacy
A legend in our skin
Carried by the children who lived it
Glistening like lightning in the desert sand

YVONNE M. ESTRADA

The Coyotes in the Living Room

The new park is done,
seamless sod rolled up against
the suburban wildland-interface.

The tricksters make us believe
there's a meadow alongside a body
of water alongside a boulevard of cars.

Little girls in fairy costumes,
one boy spins a kite in the breeze,
Sage-scrub backdrop, mostly gone.

Parade of joggers and walkers stop
to witness a shrieking woman
run down a little slope near some bushes

after her little bred-to-fit-in-a-purse dog
had been caught but released
by a coyote that had nowhere left to hunt.

Everyone who saw the mistake it had made,
knew how hungry it must have been.

I whispered to it, "Hide for now, run later."

YVONNE M. ESTRADA

My Name on Top of Yours, #14

Oh he's too high to shout, or hide, or run,
he's pinned under the ghetto-bird's spotlight,
then unfreezes, drops the bag and it's on,
he bolts past squad-cars, escapes into night.
Torn pocket and blue under fingernails,
help him tell the story all the next day,
homies in dead cars go over details,
migrate inside to play World of Warcraft,
any motivation goes up in smoke,
their boredom rolls downhill getting bigger,
they feel it close in, they know it's no joke
they're not at work, they're not in jail either,
they're just taggers, each one has what he has,
a long name on a freeway overpass.

ERIC EZTLI

A Different Doorway

Earth colored men
with paint sketched
along their skin
grab black stone blades
to slit their wrists
at the edge of a cliff
overlooking a sea
with hundreds of ships.

The rivers of blood
flood open
to become one
in mother earth.
Each drop
of ancient secrets
feeds the thirsty black dirt
for the sun has told them
that white man is coming
with El Dorado marked
in his eye.

RICH FERGUSON
When Called in for Questioning

When asked about the scars around your lips, tell them you were speaking peace in a shattered-glass world. When asked about employment, say you are a wound collector on the broken frontier. As for where you reside, tell them your heart is equidistant from joy and suffering, the now and never, the sweet flower and the Hiroshima cloud. Regarding why you say the things you say, tell them the full moon is in your mouth. When asked about the ghosts behind your eyes, say you occasionally spend too much time thinking about who you are to become, rather than who you are supposed to be. As for why some leave the world too soon, say death's reflexes are sometimes quicker than prayer.

RICH FERGUSON

A Worry Bead, a Blessing

From the deep blues of my mother's belly
I screamed my way to birth light.
Was branded with a name
passed down through ten generations
of midnight.
My mother cradled me in her arms,
gently pressed her lips to my ear.

She told me I'd been born
into a world of bombs & birdsongs,
diseases & deities, poverty & purity.

My mother said we humans are
the bold electricity of kisses,
and screams stuffed with
the latest news headlines.
We are correctly tied shoelaces
and busted hinges.
Healed wounds and broken mirrors.

She wrung ten sad songs
from the ghost in me,
then handed me over
to the brass-knuckled moon.
It pummeled me to sleep
with a thug's lullaby.

In dreamland, I didn't count fleeting sheep,
just heavy shadows.

As I grew, optimism became a consequence
of me having a wishbone ribcage.
Some days, those wishbones have broken

to the side of good fortune.
Other times, I've been left wailing
my birth-given blues.
Nightly, I shed my heavy shadow
beneath a hanging tree.
Nightly, I count the stars
in the night sky.

Each one: a worry bead.
Each one: a blessing

JAMIE ASAYE FITZGERALD
The Night Nurse

Tenderness burns like an injection
as milk comes down from under arms
into my breasts. Pearly droplets
leap out like tears, a small river flows
over my chest into the bed, the sheets
gathered around her for comfort.

The arrowhead of this love cuts.
When I wake to its exquisite pressure,
she is there for me, her hand fluttering
about my bosom in the dark, her mouth
a salve, ready to take.

JAMIE ASAYE FITZGERALD
The Voyage or Comparative Snapshots of My Father's Brain

There is shrinkage, a normal result.

We are not talking about shirts.

Not only shrinkage, but a small cerebellum stroke.

See that dark spot?

lack of movement in his left arm.

Now we are talking about shirts.

I have to pick one out,
decide between seersucker or sateen,

button-down or polo, something
to drape over his shrunken frame.

"I am on a great voyage"

and he needs the right clothes—
not shorts that fall and pool at his ankles.

When the nurse turns him sideways
to wipe his ass I try to think of him
as my daughter, my baby, to no avail:

He's my father,
who circumnavigated death

to come back to us.

ANGELA ROSE FLORES

Like My Mother

I arise with the sun
Like my grandma always does
She loves me like my mother—
Close and warm

The rooster's bugle call
Has broken the night's starry shell—
I sit up bleary eyed and unfocused
In my grandma's bed

My small feet flatten the large bubbles
On the cold yellowed linoleum—
They follow the aroma of *familia*,
History, love, caring, and dedication
Into her sanctuary

Her body sways with a rhythm
Her arms move like she's conducting
A Symphony—
She steps with movement
Like she's dancing the Fox Trot
While she hums softly
In wavering vibrato

I stand right behind her
My nose touching the apron knot
Tied on her back—
And smell her scent

She is made of love
She is made of virtue
She is made of giving
She is made of strength

Her gray hair is curled up in bobby pins
Her slippers are worn but still have
The pink bows intact
She looks over her shoulder
Down at me—
And smiles

Hands caked with flour
She presents a freshly-made tortilla
Rolled up and hot—
It is filled with liquid gold
The kind that drips out of the bottom

Someday I will be a grandma
I will love with a mother's love
Dancing in my sanctuary
Just like my grandma…
Someday

MICHAEL C. FORD
Closing Prayer

Art farther out than Heaven
Hollow be thy blame
Thy Kingdom's gone: shuddering ghost underground
Reverb in the earth (as it is in Heaven) because
  the world turns on its endangered axis,
  like a gashed tetherball
We become contrite, penitential, almost monastic
Give up this day and take away our daily bread, too
And, please, forgive trespassers, as we forgive
roadside billboard seductions
   leading us not into temptation, but
       I-Pod lobotomy
Forgive photographs of cartoony women
As subtle assemblage on our walls
  they are the only portholes
  on our sinking boat
Forgive us, Los Angeles, as we
  forgive those who Los Angeles against us;
  and lead us not into Los Angeles,
  but deliver us from Los Angeles
Omen!

MARIANA FRANCO
Night 1

My lover has the wildlife sleeping
inside his nose.
There is a grizzly bear rumbling out
from his left nostril
and a white wolf bellowing out
from his right.

At odd rare nights a banshee shrieks
from deep down his throat.
I always wake up to those
high pitch screeches
with eyes
wide open.

Two love birds have moved in
on the tip of his nose.
They sound like an inverted whistle
"Phew—phew,"
bringing me to the present.

I am grateful for his soundful distractions that
silence
my traffic jumbling thoughts.
Lying next to my lover
smiling
I sleep with him and the wildlife inside his nose.

JERRY GARCIA

Interstate 60

I saw my neighborhoods destroyed by destiny, when I was six years old.
   My friends disappeared for life, reduced to the fine powder of demolition.
   I watched their houses splintered and smashed to host an eight-lane highway.

I played with the long boards, the broken porcelain of sinks and toilets,
   cinder block perimeters, cracked foundations, silt and rusty pipe
   when water no longer flowed from homes of childhood friends.

Basement cards and jacks covered by weeds, toys traded for rock piles,
     chain-linked fences, bulldozers and cranes.
   Mortar applied, covered by black sticky asphalt, the bitter odor
    that permeated the nights of my youth.

The freeway emerged, surf and gulls in the speed of traffic, squeal of brakes
     trucks gusting a new era.
   Highways separated east from north of east,
   the immigrant Russian replaced by the middle-class Mexican-American
   replaced by new immigrant Chinese.

A skinny sixteen-year-old boy stared through concrete pylons.
   Boisterous pals, cigars and joints, became the interior of a teenage night.
   Heading west to music, tie-dye, unwashed hair, smoking and spilling wine
    on the roots buried underneath that freeway.

Ocean waves head like schooners of beer, a blue yacht background
   to the destitute of Main Street
   the homeless have disappeared or wished they had.
    99-cent movie halls, collapsed apartments and vendor shacks flattened
    to make way for malls of fast food and plastic fashion.

Street square and parallel like an engineer's grid, but I cannot drive straight.
    Noises in my head pierce sharper than squealing traffic, louder than the
        motor's torque.
    I must shift gears and exit this junkie-fueled existence before I too disappear.

Freeways don't cross cemeteries but swerve around
    thoughts waver like bad movies in a dark arcade.
    Under a freeway buttress, throat dry, breath caught as if my last,
        I purge fear of the miles and reach to rev my engine forward.

JERRY GARCIA

Downwind from a Man Sleeping in His Own Puddle

Lipsticked cigarette butts
high-roller cigars
spent condoms
and green shards
from a broken jug
of *apple wine*
wait with me
for the traffic light
to change.

On a bus bench lays
a pile of threads and bones.
The stale smell of urine
makes me fear the post-dawn chill.
Vagrants will rise to beat me
rob me of charge cards, ring, wristwatch,
and thirty-two dollars cash.

But the drifter sleeps alone, he snores.
Low winds waft his stench my way.
Detached leaves
scatter over the sidewalk.
I arrest my fright.

The signal changes.
I look at my ring and watch
hold my wallet close.
Perhaps these possessions
are all that stand between me
and the beggar's bench.

NICOLAI GARCIA

Did You Know Sea Otters Hold Hands When They Sleep So They Don't Drift Away From Each Other?

Obviously, mental illness was a factor.
Where in nature am I considered a parasite?
I don't think our feelings could have developed any faster.

Loca, I don't know what to tell you anymore.
This is worse than not being able to sleep.
I died out in that trench; didn't come back from that war.

Not even Alexander the Grape could have predicted this.
Mammals are odd creatures. You are cold-blooded.
The moon without the stars, and me without your kiss.

I look at nice things and they fill me with hate.
There is a rage in my lantern that will never go out.
I hate it when sea otters find their perfect mate.

Love was just a word. I never understood your fears.
When things slowed down I became a giant tortoise.
And you were a butterfly drinking my tears.

NICOLAI GARCIA

A Long Drive

You wake up from a dream you can't remember.
Your heart is now a compass.
It points North and you obey.

You climb into an old car
painted by heat and smog.
You fumble with a pack of cigarettes
before turning on the engine.
Soon, hands and sweat are attached
to the steering wheel
and you're on the "I-5 to Sacramento."

As you cruise through the San Fernando Valley
you think about a woman:
the affection in her voice;
the way you tasted the galaxy on her ears;
and the dead leaves in her eyes.
You remember a couple of days, as if they were weeks.
You remember one night, as if it never ended.

Somewhere in the San Joaquin Valley,
where the sun is an oppressor,
and the smells of grapes, asparagus, and apricots
have become a permanent salad in the air,
you pull your car over
and vomit on the side of the road.

You tell your heart that he's an idiot,
then you turn the car around,
and start driving back to Los Angeles.

Somewhere up north,

a little girl is happy to have a mother
to help with math homework,
and love only her—if nobody else.
For you, there are only miles ahead
on an interstate built into the darkness,
and songs about lost love
coming from the oldies station.

MARISA URRUTIA GEDNEY

City Hall Try

City Hall Try Number One
Kind love in the quiet of the city
no *angeles* could save them or grant them their wish
Chinese man American woman
can't marry, the books say no
names can't be blended like that
what would it be, Fernandez-Chow?
Couldn't roll in the California hills
might disrupt the gold mines
or the pink moment in the every dusk sky,
seas would stop shining.

City Hall Try Number Two
She remembered being born in Mexico
generations weren't important then,
the *papel* border didn't require a lot
she was a traveler, so what?
Galloping back to her *familia* to find her birth
certificate to prove
herself not American
she demanded a change, claiming a new country, her first.

No longer *La Americana*, she showed them
they laughed: it doesn't matter sweets, only same with same,
see those two eyes and that their skin,
not
the same.

He felt
in the way
while she made lingerie,
can you picture it?
Over that little house *Placita Olvera*
steaming dragons Chinatown now.

Law of the Sea Try Number Three
If crossing didn't work, she could only think of the open ocean
another horse ride
to the port of Long Beach.

She made waves for him until they arrived
at the priest waiting at the horizon
pirating love
seagulls and sun as their witness.

MARISA URRUTIA GEDNEY
Permiso

Pastora Rios gives me permission
to call the last name of me
Mexican. When she married,
Clarence, who fled California,
turned into

Claro.

She taught him how to be,
in Spanish.
Not years of conquest, just love
in the late 1800s.

She signed documents *Pastora de Gedney*
in pictures her dark skin shows, daughters with red hair
just like my dad.
I want to know if she was proud to have an English husband
or was he just American
American of English decent? *Americano?* Englishman?
The man who ran away
maybe that was it,
there were no names for it or him or her.

Isaura did as she was told—turned into Sara
but her big hips held some fight.
Yolanda just let me be.
Both with red lips fancying
want
more
thinking of far away
plotting
how to get out.

Third generation
or six generations when you count
what happened at the same time
they laid down
suffering over the kitchen sink,
body worry.
Will there be anything to cook tonight?

Giving the almost-twin boys exactly the same things,
didn't know they had nothing.
When they voted to stay or go, to leave him and start new or stay
inside the fear, hiding
sometimes
getting loud to tell him where to go—
hell isn't too far away for a seven year old.
She gave them a say,
so they decided with permission

and with it he stopped
turned back into

clean
clear
claro

permission to be new.

DANA GIOIA

Meet Me at the Lighthouse

Meet me at the Lighthouse in Hermosa Beach,
That shabby, squat nightclub on its foggy pier.
Let's aim for the summer of '71,
When all of our friends were young and immortal.

I'll pick up the cover charge, find us a table,
And order a round of their watery drinks.
Let's savor the smoke of that sinister century,
Perfume of tobacco in the tangy salt air.

The crowd will be quiet—only ghosts at the bar—
So you, old friend, won't feel out of place.
You need a night out from that dim subdivision.
Tell Mr. Bones you'll be back before dawn.

The club has booked the best talent in Tartarus.
Gerry, Cannonball, Hampton, and Stan,
With Chet and Art, those gorgeous greenhorns—
The swinging-masters of our West Coast soul.

Let the All-Stars shine from that jerrybuilt stage.
Let their high notes shimmer above the cold waves.
Time and the tide are counting the beats.
Death the collector is keeping the tab.

LIZ GONZÁLEZ

Buñuelos

Grandma stands at the kitchen counter
like a *luchador* in an apron, ready for a match.
She slaps stretched dough onto its back,
rolls a hacked-off broomstick over the top,
twists to the stove and slides
the full-moon tortilla into an iron pan.
Boiling oil swallows, spits, hisses
until the tortilla blisters, crisps.
She dips her pincher fingers in quick,
snatches the crunchy wafer from its bath,
flips it onto a paper-towel-lined plate,
slathers the top with cinnamon-*piloncillo* syrup,
and plops the sweet treat on the plastic
pink placemat in front of me. I blow on it,
pick it up with both hands, and take a bite.
The *buñuelo* breaks into twenty pieces.
I lick up the crumbs, sugar, my sticky fingers.
Grandma leaps back to the counter
for another smackdown.

WILLIAM A. GONZÁLEZ

In the Valley

To Tia Chucha's Centro Cultural & Bookstore

In the valley
There is an umbrella
Where art dances
To many unheard songs
Music instruments
Unify fingerprints
Filled with worldwide
Passion

In the valley
There is an umbrella
Where sincerity humbles
You at the front door
Books written
By many unknown writers
Stand straight up
Their words ready
To plunge through
Your pupils
Briefly scale down
Your spinal cord
Circulate lungs
Just to creep up
Into your *corazón*

In the valley
There is an umbrella
Where humanity melts
Stories frozen in time
By shining the sun
Within their own being
On top of them
Fear is unbraided
Only to be re-combed

Into straight lines
Of truth

In the valley
There is an umbrella
Where particles sleeping
Above ceiling tiles
Are blown away
By speakers
During Friday night
Open Mic events

In the valley
There is an umbrella
Where a mechanic
Can recite a
Poem written
In car oil
That still drips
From his hands
Right after work
While 500 year-old spirits
Dance to *Son Jarocho*
In the background

In the valley
There is an umbrella
Where once stray children
Lost in neighborhood traps
Graduate as youth ambassadors
That will empower future
Generations to come

In the valley
There is an umbrella
Where those who
Once drowned in misery
Today swim within
Circles of self-healing
Creations

DOROTHY RANDALL GRAY

Sandy in the Streets

TO MY SKID ROW WRITING CLASS

Hurricane Sandy
New York City drowning in debris
Wall Street hit by walls of waves
Hopes washed away
Houses burned to bits
Seaside rollercoaster rode out to sea
No power, no food, no gas, no way
To make life move again

Sandy on the streets of L.A.
Hurricanes with no names
    roaming these streets
Dragging dreams out to sea
Burning through lives that were
    until they weren't

Sandy souls picking through
    cinders of themselves
Salvaging dreams from debris
Finding what remained was still precious

Taking pen and power in hand
    they pushed past hurricanes
Swam, crawled, doggie-paddled
    through walls and waves
    fear and pain
Stroke by stroke, story by story
    they swam to shore
And wrote themselves down
    to stand upright again

Became like the moon
    moving their own tides
    and life forward once more
Shouting to all who'd listen
"Hey Sandy, I'm still here…
    I'm still here…
    I'm still here!"

ROBERT GRIBBIN

The Man in 702

He had taken a room in
    one of the luxury
hotels lining the beach
    on a high floor with a
huge picture window facing
      the sea

He remained in his room
    took all his meals there
going down to the lobby
            only to enable
the maids to tidy up and
    make his bed

Though he had brought some
    books, he did not read

He lay on the bed,
    unable to focus on a thought
occasionally dozing

        he sat for hours at the window
            looking
toward the sea

PETER J HARRIS
Baby Talk

glimpse a child's blasé rending of dimensions   witness the shape-shifting
delight of a toddler shouting to her mother: 'mama it's Mickey Mouse!'
shame on eyes that cannot see cartoon ears sprouting from the grain at
wooden interlock of hexagonal cocktail tables in a hotel lobby

savor squeal of 3-year-old granddaughter high in a playground swing
& her unstrained dismissal of chronology:
'when you were little I used to push you on the swing'

aha to the brash logic of her 4-year-old cousin:
'I think *I'm fast, then I know I'm fast*'

childhood is fragrance not my destination
my see saw made of precision & revelations in the night
my lover's fetal curl & breathing under cover of urban darkness
mi sueño spiced by lost attempts to make meaning from our baby talk
Mi susurro unfolding

Monk on *Mysterioso*
Lord have mercy of daddy's imaginary keynote at million man march
salsa of tires prowling streets soaked by sudden rain
timbales on the canopy sheltering the midnight hour

Evidence

my half-life spent
shuddering in your arms
pleasure so old
you got to carbon date it
so familiar it wears your fingerprints
stirring me like Dracula sensing sundown
twisting me like a *Cirque du Soleil* daredevil

               sanctuary between your sculpted legs
hypnotizing V & honed naked feet
trapdoor of your hips
tucking me up next to your womb

               release unleashed
                shredding me
molecules leaking
savor my percolation
lace hands with me
kiss away frown mussing my forehead
while I sway inside wind behind my ears

               I am your evidence

babbling newborn/incoherent grown man
quivering on borderline of your skin
stranded without camouflage or citizenship
tears cushion my fluttering eyes
cacophony outline my feline body
translated only by your
whispered awe & satisfied *yes yes yes*

HAZEL CLAYTON HARRISON

Sonny

Sonny was old school
The type of man who didn't stand out in a crowd
but you knew he was there
A man who liked to work with his hands
he repaired his own cars and his own house
grew his own vegetables
he even made his own wine
We called it *Sonniac*

Every now and then he'd show up at my back door
a bag of collard greens and a bottle of Sonniac in his hands
In the kitchen we'd sip his wine and talk about old times
When he left, I'd cook the greens
laughing about some story he'd shared

The last time he came by he brought sad news
"I got lung cancer," he said.
"Doctor says I only got 3 months to live."
We sat quiet for a long time that day

The next week I went by his house
He stopped working in his yard
long enough to pour me a glass of Sonniac
I sipped it slowly
The taste still lingers sweet
on my tongue.

KEVIN JAMES HEARLE

Water and Power

"IT IS TRUE THAT NEARLY 40 PERCENT OF LOS ANGELES' WATER GOES FOR
OUTSIDE USES SUCH AS LAWNS, GARDENS, SWIMMING POOLS, AND PUBLIC
PARKS... BUT SUCH AMENITIES ARE AT THE HEART OF LOS ANGELES' WAY OF
LIFE."
—REMI NADEAU

Despite your thousand pious gigolo suburbs;
and even though I know the lies the angels tell the living
in Los Angeles—the way history eclipses history here
and passes into fable—this is my heritage: the land of the lawn
and the home of the sprinkler head. Oh, I have wasted my time
detesting the soap kings and the chewing gum barons—
so much time on the real estate men planning their floral parades
and football games. They were nothing;
each one mortal and pitiful. It is the lawn which has survived,
and which I hate. I do not think they would have come—
the bacon and ham millionaires of Illinois,
the five and dime rich merchants of Ohio—if
there hadn't been lawns for the making. Without dichondra
they would not have boarded the Pullman cars for Pasadena
or Santa Barbara. If not for the sprinkler heads,
which made an arid land seem green and neatly divisible,
the railroad speculators could not have brought Iowa west,
in square lots, to the Pacific. And, without the millions
from Cedar Falls and Council Bluffs and Keokuk,
the banks would not have come—like locusts over Egypt—
with their New Yorkers spreading legends of a lost city
of true intelligence, benevolence, culture
and pastrami. The apostles of the Empire State
rehearsing their litany of things which were *better back there*,
but entering their whiny exile in ever greater numbers,
and each one wanting lawns. Never mind the seasons without rain
or the water wasted on St. Augustine; they must have lawns.
Lawns, so the people, we, the people, can move on,
(each moving van an absolution) believing

in new towns whose names sound more chaste—"Mission Viejo";
in off-ramps more green—"Ventura," "Garden Grove";
and, in—"Salsipuedes," "Los Feliz"—lives perhaps
more sibilant than what we've left behind.
Damn the lawns. Damn the sprinkler heads that feed them.
Damn the pipes and aqueducts that feed the sprinklers
that feed the lawns that feed the thirst for green and land,
and damn the dams which feed on river valleys so far away
voracious angels need never dream they once were green.

KEVIN JAMES HEARLE

The Politics of Memory

I was born in a state
where everything had to be named twice
to survive:
where Hangtown became Placerville,
where La Brea couldn't hold its bones
in Spanish, but had to be redundant
and bi-lingual—
The La Brea Tar Pits,
redundant, like the Sierra Nevada Mountains,
in name only;

a state so arid in parts
that what has been forgotten
is blown to dust
in the wind across the alkali flats;
a state where you change the name
and all is forgiven:
where Gospel Swamp
loses both its muck and its religion
to emerge the model suburb.

Fountain Valley forgives the swamp,
but what of Manzanar?
In a state where everything
has to be named twice
or be forgotten,
who will remember Manzanar
(a place in exile
from the maps)? The detention camp is closed,
but I was born into this state,
and, for now, I know the name.

ADOLFO Y. HERNANDEZ
tamale hustle

it's all about the tamale hustle,
making something out of nothing.

when you don't have access to wall street,
main street,
easy street—
even though
you're a rent check away
from living on the street.

yelling out *"tamales!,"*
with no
license, permit,
or document
legalizing
your right to existence.

yelling out *"tamales!"*
like
yelling out "fire!"
—"fire!"—
to
anyone and everyone.

yelling out *"tamales!"*
because
yelling out for
"help!"
will get you nowhere.

RAUL HERRERA

Earthquakes

In 1906, an 8.2 sized earthquake ruptured the San Andreas Fault, killing an estimated 3,000 people.

If vibrations break boulders and devastate lives,
Then our words can split open minds
And alter the geographical shape of its content.
Because sound is vibration our verbs are its earthquakes
And our hands are much like the Richter scale,
Charting the magnitude of our words.
So when you write, I fight the urge to destroy my enemies
Because an Earthquake named Gandhi once told me,
Even revenge has aftershocks.
That even a whisper can cause a revolution.

2010
A 7 .0 sized earthquake takes the lives
Of 300,000 Haitians.

Despite what you think I am not a natural disaster.
More like a phenomenon that's misunderstood.
Do not underestimate the Hercules behind your tongue
Your voices are the reasons this planet's axis is tilted.
But your silence is the reason this planet is dying.
So let's cause a ruckus!
If Earthquakes can destroy lives
Our voices can rebuild them.

2011
A 9.0 earthquake demolishes Fukushima, Japan
Taking the lives of 15,000.

"I have been to the mountain top and I looked over
And I've seen the promised land"
But the only thing in our way is a mute mountain.

So we crumble mountains
We crack rock without needing a pipe.
Just give me a word.
One sentence can make the ground move like a Tsunami.

You can see their words cracking the concrete
Cracking
Like the backs of the rebels from the past
Cracking
Like the blast that killed 2 Pac's laugh
Malcolm exited this world
Believing that his earthquake would cause repercussions.
"The future belongs to those who prepare for it today."

So today I have a dream
But my dream wasn't heard.
Today I have a dream
But my dream was deferred.
Today I had a dream about a king, but the king wasn't heard.
The legends are angry.
The world is violent while we stay still.
Newton's 3rd law states,
"For every action there is an equal and opposite reaction."
For example, if the action is
Division
Then the opposite reaction would be
Communication.
Problems react to solutions.
Oppression reacts to revolution.
The death of Trayvon Martin reacts to Zimmerman's execution.
Now this is law.

Voices react to vibrations,
Vibrations react to earthquakes,
So if sound is vibration our verbs are its earthquakes.
Let's break the ground our fallen heroes are trapped underneath in.
Resurrect poets from graves,
REACT
Leaders from being slayed,

REACT

Let's all speak with tremors trembling towers.
Talk like an earthquake.
Be like a rock,
And watch
This granite planet
Shake.

RAUL HERRERA
To Quentin Tarantino

I bet you sleep like a vampire.
Wake up to the sound of gunshots in the trunk of your car
While the chauffer drives you around the city.

Our city.

The city that broke you into genius,
The city that scarred your skin into roadmaps and success,
Is the same city that breaks me.

You made your sorrows into sequels,
Struggles into street chases.
You directed the funny side of gory,
The enlightening side of lost.
L.A. is heartbreaks and clichés and you made it a love story
Worth bleeding for.

You turned Japanese into Americans.
Proved that the sword is always faster than the gun
As long as it's sharpened by the best tools.
And the best fools always die last.

And you let the heroes die first if only to prove the point that life
Is no movie script.
And you can't choose your role,
And you certainly can't choose how it ends. You bend reality
So far back that you make it true.
You made an assassin out of Lucy Liu,
You made eyes pop out in Kill Bill 2
And your legacy is death-proof.
No one will ever forget about the Hanzos or the Vegas
Your legacy is death-proof.

You made a movie out of misery and made it marvelous.
You made a life out of a movie and made it true.
You made a life made of misery
And made it art.
The hardships, the pains, the worn down, the stains,
Negativity fueled your creativity.

But now L.A. streetlights are flickering,
Future DiCaprios failing their English classes,
future Foxxes without funding for the arts.
L.A. kids got potential,
And you're the greatest example.
Future directors, misdirected.
Future writers, illiterate and neglected.

Poetry has saved my life much like films have saved yours.
Art opens doors
Out of ghettos and suburbs and iron bars and stilettos.
There are kids in your city that will never get the chance
To write, or sing, or dance, or live.

I have your curiosity,
please give me your attention.

Listen to a boy from Alhambra create legends with his words.
Listen to a girl from Crenshaw create roads with her hands.
Listen to schools with no programs (just exams)
Create millennium trilogies.
Come watch us burn down the theater like Julie Dreyfus.
The inglorious glory of Los Angeles's stories
Are begging for you to listen.
We're waiting for your sunlight like dusk till dawn.
The camera is on your city.

I have your curiosity.
Please give me your attention.
Watch our legacy
Become death-proof.

WILLIAM RYAN HILARY

How to Sell Your First Screenplay and Become Rich

1.

Find the child
Inside
Who'll come to despise you.

2.

Watch him.
Stalk him.
Stick a pin in him.
Tell his story.
Follow the thin trail
Of hair as it falls from
His head
As he ages.

3.

Follow
Over those
Dank, playground nights
Over bloody noses and fistfights
The sweats
That remind you:
"*Guilt* makes for a hell of a tale, boy"
Romance too, but romance is usually
An indelible fog—Fraud
A note clipped on the wings of a pigeon or a frog
Or a finger pressing, curled 'come-hither'
On the sweet, secret spotted insides of a woman

You barely knew, and so will be able to love forever
Because you barely knew her.

4.

Accept
Art is a re-wrapped gift.
You had it, rejected it, traded it.
Now you want to sell it.

5.

Sell it.

WILLIAM RYAN HILARY

Poems from the Bargain Bin

I notice in pretty restaurants,
Erotic games and children's toys;
The flakes of my disease.

For I am often baroque with my verbiage,
Stacking too many too high,
Too little too low.

My pulse lives in words,
Though my spirits rise with wine,
Because I am weak and lack in wealth
Come from a quiet family,
And have not suffered enough.

Often before an altar of electric light,
Working upon plastic papyrus,
I wonder if I tug as hard at the seams of others
As I do my own.

When stung by their sadness,
When retching at their ruptures,
I touch bruises, or scrape
The inner rawness'
Of women and men
Who I love from afar,
But detest in intimacy

Then alone in their pain;
I find I am a stranger to my own.

MARLENE HITT

Child on a Floor with Marble

From the floor, peering into it,
the cat's eye seems larger
than his sister's sweater
lying on the sofa, larger
than the moon outside.
One small marble
in one small hand
eclipses the window, even a door.
In lamplight the cat's eye,
set deep, glows orange
and alive, a pinpoint
of eerie other worlds.
As the child's eye closes
he sees the center glowing
fire-like and the glass rolling
down a narrow hallway
to an open door, glass,
open a mere crack,
inviting, maybe, freedom.
In dreaming his body sweats
while he rolls unfettered,
unbound, free, sliding,
slipping further down in dream
until the gentle tap;
"Son, come to bed now"
and the sting of lost dreams hurts.
Sleep returns, deep and healing
not orange, just black.
In the marble's world
the cat's eye lies sleeping,
lost somewhere on the edge
of the front room carpet
at the edge of outside.

MARLENE HITT

Big Thunder

In the old days the settlers
thought Tujunga meant
"Big Thunder,"
for when the boulders
washed down the canyon walls
the roars of great storms echoed
matching the tone
of the thunder from the sky.
The river would rise
widening the canyon
washing away the lodges,
the Boy Scout Camp,
the swimming holes.
One year a piano floated downstream
homes filled with mud.
In 'seventy-eight the coffins
washed a mile down into town.
Big Thunder.
When the sun beat down
all that rain seeped low
into the underground
like it has run away
ashamed of itself,
ran into a great hidden lake
deep under the rocks
which they named "Pasko"
after a preacher.
Sagebrush and dry sand whistled away
into the "Santanas"
as though nothing like rain had happened.
Oh that rain! It poured with its steady sound,
moved the rock, moved the ground.
Yes, Big Thunder, when canyon walls echoed,
when boulders plowed down and down
to deepen the valley floor.

JEN HOFER

Resolve

The liquid light liquefies everything it touches, which is
everything, making the opposite of halos, which is the exact
outline of things against their backdrop of sky or wall of tree,
which is another way of conjugating, which if we didn't know
better we might call "clench" or "decline" but instead agree
to agree by the river confluence.

Tasks amass, waiting amasses, tree-tops, cement swales, outsized
scripts, manmade urban nature, bail bondsmen, kick-out panels
in institutionalized doors amass, stairwells and double-wide
trailers and "why didn't i think of this ten years ago" and gun
lockers and guns and long keys worn on regulation-issue belts
amass, visiting prisoners in lock-up where we too are locked up
until we are prioritized, as "this door will be opened according
to the priorities of the moment."

A doorway a bond pursuits against the war laws instinct
accelerated cultivation in which to puppet depict flame procure
transmit we variegated we metropolis we Angelenos we adapt
we sentiment we defiance we undisclosed discernible reality
formalized for the sake of warmth on a rainy day.

Elm Street, Carson Civic Center, Museum of Jurassic Technology,
Center for Land Use Interpretation, Century Boulevard Denny's
Parking Lot, LAX, Les Figues Headquarters, upstairs apartment
corner of Pasadena Avenue and Avenue 34, Elm Street, emptied
out atomic hurtle along the rails of a system long defunct or
unaware of our surroundings we are surrounded.

Two kinds of guava, both equally fragrant, two kinds of
persimmon, one eaten crisp, the other eaten exceedingly soft.

ALEXANDRA HOHMANN

The Brown Girl in Her

INSPIRED BY LUIVETTE RESTO'S "THE WHITE GIRL IN HER"

Her skin was darker as a child,
skin that tanned instead of burned.

Her hair was Other,
grew in unwanted places, forearms and face,
thick and dark as *mole*,
distinctive and unwanted amongst blonde, blonde cousins.

The white girl
is supposed to flash a toothy smile,
get good grades,
buy makeup labeled "ivory,"
own records by Taylor Swift.

Instead the brown girl
listens to the rhythms of *cumbias y rancheras*,
eager to dance
(though the white girl in her has two left feet).
The brown girl
feels guilty for not understanding what she reads in Spanish;
her European heritage betrays her Latin tongue
as she struggles to pronounce her double r's.

The wanna-be brown girl
hasn't been south of the border,
doesn't know where in Mexico she comes from,
hasn't smelled ancestral earth or ground cornmeal for *tortillas*.

The white girl
who teaches little brown children all day
isn't brown enough to say
"*Sientese, por favor*"
without being met with mocking laughter.

They don't know what courses through her veins,
her grandfather's *machismo*,
grandmother's pride,
homemade *tamales* fueling her Chicana soul.

ALEXANDRA HOHMANN

This Small Thing

This small thing—
once hot coals left unattended,
chicken bone boiling in broth,
peeling wallpaper in an abandoned room—
surges from the pit of my stomach,
climbs my esophagus,
leaps out of my mouth,

sin vergüenza.

This small thing demands to be heard,
doesn't need no ransom,
wants walls to bounce off,
ears to fill,
minds to change.

This small thing
wants freedom
laughter
joy
heartache
refuses to be suppressed any longer.

BORIS SALVADOR INGLES

all the characters

driving along main
w/ my father

i remember watching
all the players

pace
peddle
pushing along
in wanton whisper

heavy
hideous
hoarders

main-line-junkies
slamming
chiva blanca

parasites
propagating
their lust
for life

my father called it
la tristeza
del vicio

he'd say
this is where
they all end

these
expatriates
of life

these lost
vacuous
souls

all
rotting
along
the curb

BORIS SALVADOR INGLES

evergreen head stones

walking barefoot
over cold
serrated
blades

i discover the dead
are still learning to die

la duena still knits
chisme on her stoop
& tends to her garden

el dueno hides in the mist
of his country memory
swinging like a plume
in his *maca*

singing bibulous
a cappella

up on old brooklyn
maria trembles in & out
of slamming doors
rolling nickel-bags
in the crooks of her arms

drifting
infinitely

the only quiet ones
are the unattended
the unmarked
the unknown

they spend most days
waiting on kind words
lying face down
against the earth

gnawing their smiles
through their cheeks

GERDA GOVINE ITUARTE

Part I, 44 Days

GLOBALPOST CORRESPONDENT JAMES FOLEY WAS KILLED ON AUGUST 19,
2014 BY ISLAMIC STATE MILITANTS IN SYRIA, WHERE HE HAD BEEN HELD FOR
CLOSE TO TWO YEARS. IN 2011, JAMES FOLEY SPENT 44 DAYS IN CAPTIVITY
INSIDE MUAMMAR GADDAFI'S LIBYA. HE WROTE FIVE CHAPTERS TO TELL HIS
STORY. THIS POEM IS THE FIRST OF FIVE THAT TRACKS HIS JOURNEY DURING
THE 44 DAYS.

I am on board
teenage boys drive
to the last checkpoint
scan road front line up ahead
rebel trucks behind
no one speaks   get out of vehicle

crawl | speeds up
like schools of fish that
hunted together but with no
clear leader or command structure
eyes dart   nervous
guts taunt   risk on steroids

threads of the know unravel
suddenly trucks barrel downhill
machine guns spray bullets
ak 47 rounds whiz over head
I crawl forward toward a larger
sand dune with my camera rolling

some journalist said
libya was the perfect war
they were able to get close
but not too close
to hear the mortar fire
smell the black smoke from incinerated

trucks and sometimes burned flesh
by evening connect to internet
send in their stories in the
comfort of the Benghazi hotel
reality smirked
learned no perfection in war

led by young people
hopeful | fire in their bellies
brain dry cleaned
ignorance & survival collide
blindfolds inhumane treatment
punishment runs rampant

daily drill |oppress|manipulate
lie| confuse| own| squeeze out confession
reporting was my job
frontlines felt normal.

160

GERDA GOVINE ITUARTE

Poster Boy

A 12-YEAR-OLD BOY SOLDIER WAS ASKED WHAT HE MISSED THE MOST
AFTER HE WAS RESCUED. HE SAID, "WHEN I HAD A GUN I NEVER HAD TO
WORRY ABOUT FOOD."

Sweet faced boy in a green bandanna.
Hair in his face. Covering his eyes.

His fingers clutch an ice cream cone.
Pistachio. A strawberry on top.

AK 47 leans into him.
He leans into the camera.
The ice cream melting.

Rain

it gets much too dry in
L.A.

so i called out for the weather to
change

or at least, i wrote to you for
it

just yesterday, as a matter of
fact

and i don't believe in
coincidence

granted, i simply acknowledged my
method

waiting for haphazard
showers

to come and clean my
car

this car i drive that once was
yours

don't think i forgot, i do vividly
recall

you relayed two simple
requests to me

time and time
again

Keep the car
clean.

Visit me at my
grave.

i am terrible at
both

so you answered with
rain

TRACI KATO-KIRIYAMA

Pilgrimage to the Meaning of Ash

(PARTS 1 & 2 OF A SERIES)

part 1 -

Crenshaw exit off the 405 in North Torrance:
  next door to the Coffee Bean where I write
  down the street from Ma's old high school
  the exact point where the government told Grandpa
he would be removed from his life at their whim
they told him freeways needed exits
all Grandpa could utter was
Again
concrete pillars plowed through his blood that fed their land
and quelled the guts from the *shigin* he used to sing
the rest of his thoughts, locked
between a bottle of *sake*
and the soil in his palm,

where ash turns to stone

——

part 2 -

we go all the way to Manzanar in April to make Pilgrimage
past the plots of land dotting every freeway, highway, airport
where grandpa, auntie, uncle, grandma, dad, made their
way as farmers, nurserymen, gardeners
where they plowed, seeded, planted, sang into soil, grew
where they were born, ripped, replaced, razed from soil, buried
they lay now in the peaceful part of earth they never got to see
under cemetery plaques that don't do justice to what they engraved
i bring them cut flowers that would make them turn in their plots
my eyes carve new inscriptions into granite every time i visit
i try to hear them sing and laugh, try to regurgitate their guttural pride,
try to show them the new intersections we have come to map, lines

of spirits drawn next to the others before them, where removals
turned the soil of reservations, where they were all meant to be forgotten,
where we pledge that will never happen, where we make sense of pilgrimage

where ash turns the stone

DOUGLAS KEARNEY

-ING

it's a flight path up and out for 'em.
departure to be out for the up.
white clouds on a dungaree up
on some flight.   rrrrrrrrrrrrr some path
out for the up white rides out on a fast
departure to the out. a flight path
                    rrrrrrrrrrrrrrrrr 'waul the steel gulls
of belly full of flight, steel gulls
smoke the dungaree sky up.
yellow clouds on an acid wash
the white out.   rrrrrrrrrrrrrrrr arrivals to the in.
gulls? naw uh, naw uh a bus. naw uh, naw uh
bucks. leaned with boxes, an Impala a buck. a Buick.
                    rrrrrrrrrrrrrrrrrrrrrr a flight path
dungs the block. boxes, chock up with the in.
gulls block the dungaree up, an unkindness of flight.
a path blocked. bucks in bucks buck on blocks, low flight.
                    rrrrrrrrr a bus belly full of arrival,
departure. smoke clouds the low path.
                    rrrrrrrrrrrrrrrrrrrr the Forum chocks the blocks up,
no path for Buicks, Impalas. wall to wall 'waul of cars,
trucks, buses from out on in. the path full full full.
fabulous for 'em, the up-and-in-from-out. the-down-
and-out-and-in   rrrrrrrrrrrrrrrrrrrrrr a block blocked.
man! a flight path steel gulls like gull dung
on the yellow wash dungaree sky
                    rrrrrrrrrrrrrrrrrrr tickets? tickets?
got no tickets. no departure.
steel bucks the blocks down. up, the gulls like
a murder of flight. naw! naw! naw!
                    rrrrrrrrrrrrrrrr low lows on arrival,
the block chocked.
no path for Buicks, Impalas, low lows now naw uh, naw uh,

naw uh. wall to wall 'waul of cars, trucks,
buses from out on in. block the path. man!
fabulous for 'em, the up-and-in-from-out.
                rrrrrrrrrrrrrrrrrrr the-down-and-out-and-in
inaw! inaw! inaw! blocks deep. the Forum gone
dark as the dark blocks bucked up, white smoke
on a rival Impala, low low—buck! buck! buck!
the 'waul! boxes full up. the fulvous up gulps
the steel gulls out and in. hawks up copters, choppers
hawk the dungaree sky up and down the path. man!
                rrrrrrrrrrrrr hawk the blocks, fill up boxes
with Impalas and low lows. wash the down-and-
out-and-in out. fabulous departures for 'em!
fixing to unblock a flight path for the up-and-in-from-out in.
fabulous arrivals! back back back. the Forum,
dark, till Eagles! Eagles! Eagles! you can check in
watch watch watch up for the white clouds' slow arrival.
      you can   rrrrrrrrrrrrr leave

KAREN KEVORKIAN

The Proofreader Raises Hands to Eyes Without Anyone Seeing

Like a Sunday morning, wet drips from a tree fern, a palmetto's fingertips
scrabble, a string quartet on the radio saws morning in half

regimes of the legible in the fanned pages of the fat news, acetylene rat tat

in the throat of a crow whose feathers are not lustrous with secretive purple
and patent but the inarticulate black of old coffee

water pulses down gutters on either side of the street though no water in
the taps

at the end of the block steam hammers chatter, winter in the mind but not
the patrician winter of poetry

in Arabic and Armenian neon blur of alphabet on deli plate glass, chande-
lier waterfalls to electrify noon, not the green silk of an underground river

around, across, returning, liquid cursive beneath streets' gridded logic

the marine layer forms over coastline the tall skinny palms needle, fog slips
down a window

pools on a sill, a sky of pewter then steel, hard shades of gray, six thousand
readers buy the book of a Christian named Pearl who writes children
should be hit to train them

although to strike in anger is wrong, though not wrong to hit a six-month-
old, it is necessary to show the child its error

a plastic cord will not damage muscle or tissue, a cat tears out little feathers

KAREN KEVORKIAN

Our Lady of Sorrows or is it Solitude

Each day contrives a new architecture of pillows,
letters smoothed flat, bent photos, notes on yellow paper

whole years forgotten, not necessarily important ones

smudge by the door, blue clad figure hovering,
from the corner nattering, a child that mumbles

out of adult hearing, the voice always fictitious,
hissy sibilants, trees shushing, shudder and surge

stubby pile of the almost velvet chair that looked smooth,
prickles

8:30 p.m., too little light, cat leads the way, disappears
in gloom just above the floor

sensation of movement is what a ghost is, worn sheets
and all the feet shoved at the end of them

DOUG KNOTT
Home Movie in Green and White

The pale house with the green shutters open
Let the afternoon sun into the room
Where I hit my sister in the head
With a baseball bat
Not during the official season
But during the eternal season of the child

Shutters agape, the ball flew out
Like a random pistol shot
That yet held the whole house hostage;
The windows shook like birdcages
With feathers dropping on the lawn
I foolishly tried to hang on inside
Aftershocks lasted for years

The sloping bluegrass lawn fell down
Before the street; my father
Rolled down the new-mown grass, drunk
With the neighbor's wife in his arms
Both of them laughing
Covered with little green blades

I put the baseball bat back in the closet
And the house settled on a new foundation
Slightly closer to hell

DOUG KNOTT
The Laughing Wall

In Jerusalem, the Wailing Wall
Is large, strong, and very tall.
It's popular with weeping crowds and package tours

But down the road a bit is another wall
Far older, overgrown
And rather small
It's called:
           the laughing wall

There, every day, the best
Comedians of the human race
Go out face to face
With Goliath!

The stones absorb their punch lines
And grow warm
In the sunset of the world

The package tours and weeping crowds
Ignore this little wall,
Which, after all,
Is old, overgrown
And rather
small

HALEY LANINGHAM

A Year of Being Both Gay and Religious

"Repent, repent, repent,"
I called from the gutters of Santa Monica Boulevard, but in secret
I zipped up my coat, tightened my tie,
buttoned my dress, laced up my boots,
and thought about whom I thought
and dreamt about what I dreamt.
Sometimes I felt I should fix it,
and sometimes I felt there was nothing to fix.
Whoever told me there was something to fix?
Then finally I stepped out into that same street,
and that night I sinned so sincerely
that it meant more to me than all the hours spent pleading Him
or those mornings spent sobbing in the pews;
those wooden slides
to wherever damnation was, and is, and is to come
were always too slick and shiny to keep my twisted soul, anyway.
The child in me tried to clamber up them,
made a game of it, "The Floor is Lava,"
but those slippery rainbow socks just wouldn't come off.
These nights, her hand on my shoulder,
the crying eyes of the damned
seem more fearfully and wonderfully made than stained glass disciples
turning my face red and green in the pews.
For now I am older, and at peace.
But although I am done with the years of me
for which I was not present,
and although I have sung every praise I will have ever sung,
there is always that year of me
lost in the depths of hellfire.

HALEY LANINGHAM

The Valley and Family Tectonic

"BLIND THRUST FAULT: N. A TYPE OF FAULT OR BREAK IN THE EARTH'S
CRUST THAT DOES NOT RUPTURE ALL THE WAY TO THE SURFACE SO THAT
THERE IS NO EVIDENCE OF THE SPLIT SEEN FROM ABOVE."
—FROM THE U.S. GEOLOGICAL SURVEY'S "EARTHQUAKE GLOSSARY"

In the early hours of January 17, 1994,
with Hurricane Katrina still a gleam in the eye of the Gulf,
the Northridge Earthquake shook Los Angeles awake.
The whole event only lasted about fifteen seconds, less time than a father
lets his alarm clock's measure of radio static rip into the silence of the dark
morning before breaking into his own day. This, and the Earth's crack are
both sounds you can hear from down the hall: a newscaster *in medias res*, a
flourish of mariachi brass blown into sleep, so much violent fuzz resounding
and receding in waves, his hand coming down hard on the snooze, and all the
glass falling out of the cabinets. What's important, though, is the feeling of either,
the way they halt the orbit of breaths through the rooms and rattle the
whole home.

What happened underground:
two pieces of the Earth's crust in all their jagged layers,
two plates the length of which could not be walked in a week, slid right
past each other like bricks falling from the broken foundation of the
mailbox he hit while leaving drunk, or her bare shoulder brushing his
in steps from bed to bathroom, her stone frown bending near to a break.

Hours after the quake, their marriage and every other beloved delusion
crumbled within the panic over the San Fernando Valley; I tell you
that the scoreboard over Angel Stadium fell into the stands, that
Disneyland closed down, and the set of Seinfeld, embarrassed to be there
and not, in fact, in New York, quietly halted production, but that this
didn't matter because all the boxy TVs had, for a long time thereafter,
no power anyway. These lines of electricity had crashed, too.

But, I will also tell you—as a fact—when I saw this family from across the
street praying in the dew of that morning, how the three held each other in

their front yard and gazed into a heaven Los Angeles will not see again
until all the power burns out, this time for good, perhaps only after we're
all dead and in the ground,

that bathed in the light of a million revealed stars, and in the void of 4:45AM
the round of her back draped over the warm core of their son, the father's arms
around them both like mighty rings swirled into the love of shared flesh
they were, for a moment, their own solid planet.

TEKA LARK
Choices of Heat

"It's hot and a lot of Black people"
When people discuss Lancaster,
That's what they always say—aloud.

But they whisper, "It's getting kind of bad there."

They're all moving, from L.A.
South Central, Compton, Watts.
Not too many people from Santa Monica—not any.

(It's not South Central, now it's South L.A.)

It's so Black, it looks like Mobile, Alabama.
It's so Black, it looks like Mexia, Texas.
It's so Black, it looks like your mama.

The houses are huge in Lancaster.
There's a program
"Leave your place in Jungle and get $500 extra help—to move!"

(It's not the Jungle, now it's Baldwin Village.)

You're never going to get to ride the train Auntie.
I'm scared of trains.
I'm scared of L.A., it's bad here.

It's hot, but there's a lot of Black people.
It looks like the 80s.
No, it looks more like the 60s, when I came here from the Lower Nine.

(It's not Lower Nine, now it's Holy Cross.)

Remember when me and your uncle lived in Watts?
It got real bad there.
They shot the dog, they need Jesus.

I don't remember that Auntie.
I remember that scary dog had a heart attack on Central Avenue
When a car backfired.

Why are there so many big empty houses there?
Why are there so many Black people there?
Why doesn't anyone notice how hot that place is?

It's dry heat, dry heat isn't so bad, be thankful.
You never had to be in Louisiana, picking cotton—in the summer.
You can't escape wet heat.

The houses in Lancaster are big and it's still L.A.
And the heat isn't so bad, it's dry.
If you just stay still, dry heat isn't so bad.

Random Violence

My great-great-grandfather came to Los Angeles in 1890 after taking the
opportunity of slitting his father's throat
in an act of random violence
in New Orleans.

His father—my great-great-great-grandfather had the biggest and most
luxurious home in the Garden District in New Orleans.

Some people called it a plantation.

America has always been a violent country

And Los Angeles
Has always been
a violent town.

It exists owing to murder and lies, but murders and lies open the door
for opportunities
for random violence.

In 1900 my great-great-grandfather opened a bar and out of it he sold
     as he called it
—opportunities.

Some people called him a loan shark.

Some people said my great-great-grandfather was a violent man.

My great-grandfather continued running the bar and the business of
opportunities and then gave it to my grandfather.

My grandfather used these opportunities to send my mother to UCLA and
she became the first legitimate member of the Molyneux family, but I

always liked my grandfather. I would hang out with him in the bar, help him clean his gun and help him balance his books.

One day we were walking up Central Avenue.

And a man walked up to us and attempted to grasp his opportunity.

He told my grandfather that he wanted his money.

He seemed to have a gun in his pocket.

My grandfather gave him an opportunity and asked him if he was sure and did the young man know who he was and did the young man see he was with his favorite granddaughter
the young man said, "Give me your fucking money old man."

My grandfather took out his silver gun, a gun I had pointed at my sister's head a week prior in a game of cops and robbers,
and shot him in the arm.

The young man said with disbelief, "You shot me."

And my grandfather said, "You tried to rob me and you better run, before I make it so you can't run anymore."

The young man ran away. I guess he didn't have a gun and my grandfather looked at me and said, "Beak, what did you learn." He called me Beak because my name was Lark, which is a bird and birds have beaks and I talk a lot.

I said, "That if you walk outside that people will try to rob you,"

And he said, "No, that's not the lesson. The lesson is, if you try to rob people, you will get shot."

At the bar the following week while drinking the root beer float my grandfather made me on Fridays after school
a murder in South Central
was reported on the television.

They flashed a picture of a young man who was laid out on the sidewalk
with yellow tape surrounding his body
filled with bloody holes.

The reporter said, "In a case of random violence in South Central LA a
young man was killed."

I looked over at my grandfather from the bar stool and he smiled and asked
me did I like my treat
And I smiled back
And nodded my head yes.

And that's the day I learned that you don't pull a gun on a gangster
unless you plan on killing him
and there is no such thing as
random violence.

ANTHONY A. LEE

Memory of Abel

AFTER SERGIO ORTIZ

I met Abel at the northern
corner of the Plaza in El Paso.
Thirteen years old.
Good at selling the pleasures
of the body that his demons,
northern and white, pay for cheap
while they moan the hymns
of the one-eyed siren.
In his eyes you could see
the reflections of possible johns
that night—and a little coldness.
The cold that you know is death.

My work is just work,
he said. My family is a pain. Friends?
My friends are the dollars
in my pocket. Food?
Food hurts my stomach, he whispered.

The other day, early,
I passed by the plaza
with the cheap stuff on sale,
and there I caught the smile
of a child lying on a bench—
seeing what had so long been gone.
A few tears came out, but
I don't know where they came from.
I gathered them one by one
and made a rosary of childhood
that I hoard selfishly—
that today I take out
to remember how beautiful you were,
and that makes me think of a sad
Portuguese song,
O Infante!

ANTHONY A. LEE

No Moon in L.A.

"O FOOLS, AND SLOW OF HEART TO BELIEVE ALL THAT THE PROPHETS
HAVE SPOKEN"—LUKE 24:25

just after sunset
behind me in the parking lot
as I got out of the car alone
he was talking fast
asked for two dollars
to get to Newport Beach
back to the rehab center
where he could dry out
needed to get back there
had been a drug counselor there
had been clean for a year there
celebrated with his parents
helped lots of people
a few days later
started drinking again
didn't know why
maybe just because
he had made it through
and after that there was no point
maybe some unconscious desire
to go back to his youth
his family pure Sicilian
high cheeks, chiseled chin
facial angles good enough for the screen
his father gave him
$1,500 every Monday morning
for nothing, just to spend
he and his friends wasted
all the time, a continuous party
where nothing made sense
now he was on the street

jeans filthy like a child's
after six hours of play
his brown hair tangled and greasy
glistened under street lights
he had had it
just wanted out
lifted up his shirt to show
me his ribs, dark skin
bones on a hairless chest
I stared in the almost dark
like in the Bible
my eyes opened
I saw my brother
but didn't know whether to throw
my arms around him
or kneel to kiss his hand
I gave him five dollars
Taco Bell on the left
blinked red, gold, green
the 7-Eleven next door gave out
its halo glow through the glass
how much booze
could he buy with five dollars
I wondered
how much cheap wine
two bottles maybe
one rock of coke outside the door
asphalt below us
above us just black
we stood alone together for a moment
He said, I don't have anyone to talk to
looked down, arms at his sides, palms up
I said, you don't have to tell me
any more humiliating stories
not for $5, Jesus Christ!
that was it

I wish now I had put my forehead to his shoes
I wish I had pushed his bare chest

against mine and held on
I wish I had driven him there
stayed in the rehab room
told him I loved him
gripped his shoulders when he trembled
slept in his bed
my bare arm over his naked body
wiped his face when he sweat
braced him from behind when he vomited
listened to his crazy stories
got him through detox
stayed there to see him through
not just a year, ten years, twenty—more
let him save my soul

JANICE LEE

Los Angeles

Look at the sky, I say.

I don't see anything, you say.

In this place, it is possible to be surrounded by everyone and to be completely alone. In this place, it is possible to simultaneously feel the effect of urban grunge and filth and beauty, garbage and grime in every alleyway, that smell of shellfish, that look that people give you when stopped at an intersection, to feel all of that alongside a legendary hyphen, the reciprocity of nature, of trees, of dirt, of birds, of air.

When you stretch out the transparent layers of this city, it becomes a confession.

The confession isn't the desire for death, though there is that too, but that you miss your mother.

The sun and the heat become irrelevant until you go outside to confront the light.

But in the light there is mother, there is that untraceable wound that began with birth.

The city changes when you do, and the confession is that each and every gesture becomes filled with uncertainty.

The city is so certain of itself, but it confesses that it knows nothing when there is the sky.

It's a matter of taking a few steps back, to trace the wound back to the light, the light a frantic ghost.

Not every panorama is an equal snapshot of this city, yet in the end they are all the same, confessing.

It rained once, a thoughtless nod to the wound of this city.

The neighbors yelling next door don't know to face the silence courageously.

The obligation is to pass the shadow on the sidewalk and to keep walking, to skip the embrace with light.

The proclamation is that you are an individual but in one moment you are part of a mass, in another, a ray of light.

Here is the real dilemma. That so many moments in this city are inarticulable. My confession is that I try relentlessly and hopelessly to capture moments via images, words. This is all a futile exercise. All of this only ends in failure. But sometimes, inarticulation becomes articulation. That is, the photo I try to take, the one that captures none of the essence that I felt in that very moment when I looked up at the sky and wanted to cry, could have died right there, that the photo instead becomes the articulation of that inarticulable moment in a way that the evidence can only be a frantic ghost too, a wound, a relinquishing of *everything* into a concentration of *something*.

Let me know that you get this. I mean, photos are an example of this, yes, trying to capture that sunset, that cosmic allusion to all of space and time in the upper light of the sky, that devastating miracle of life that becomes contaminated by so many small things. But other articulations too.

Like: *I love you.*

Words for one of the most inarticulable of sensations. I mean, this is not the same thing for everyone. Every *I love you* is not equivalent. There is no such thing as repetition in love, yet here are the words that claim, that attempt, that bravely endeavor to signify a specific value via language. This is as absurd as calling the sky "blue," as calling the sunset "beautiful," as claiming you feel "happy." All of these attempts, gravitations, comments: absolutely and most certainly, absurd.

But I say *I love you* and I mean it. I mean *something* that I can't describe but these words are the closest approximation, an agreed upon convention that these words will mean something close to what it is I feel, but what is important is the conjuration of all the other feelings associated with the gesture of the phrase, that when you say *I love you* I can feel this sensation of finitude and eternity in my bones, that I can feel the widening of breath, the threat of paralysis when it all ends, and an entire substantial reality built around you that does not yet exist, will never exist.

When I say *I love you*, I recall the memories of a thousand nights of presence, the limits of feelings at night when I am in my bed, when I am outside, when I pause to linger in a single moment of *existence*. Feelings reveal the taint of past trauma. Feelings become vocality and articulated via gestures. You hold my hand and for a moment, that is *everything*.

Can I confess that you become connected to this city somehow, that this city hardly existed before you, that every sky or sunset or towering building, every glamorous palm tree, every sad one, every reflection of light off a window, every conjured sound, they all begin to match the repetitive vitality of your breath, your touch, your existence. This doesn't have to make any sense. It doesn't make any sense that I know you, that you exist, *here*, with me. I'm not sure where you came from. I'm not sure when I came from either. It doesn't seem to matter, though at some point in my life, these things *did* matter. So many things mattered. What matters is your touch. Your breath. Your body next to mine. Your existence in this city with me. What matters is that suddenly, very much suddenly, I cannot imagine life without you. That is what *love* is, perhaps, a complete rearranging of the imagination, a complete infiltration of a subjectivity that seems to defer how images correlate with each other. Suddenly, what matters is the color of the sky. The direction of the stars. The speed of light. Significance and insignificance change places.

Moments in space.

The density of the fog.

It is all terrifying. One day, this city will swallow me whole, and no one, not even the pigeons, will notice.

KIMBERLY LIEU

temple

we spend hours discussing whether uncle is
a boar or a rooster.

no one knows, not his sad wife,
ruby-eyed child, or gray mother.

it is the difference of being buried
on thursday or friday

in the late fall morning or
early afternoon.

the forged papers tell a slightly different story:
55, a boar.

so it will be friday.
a second cousin or someone familiar

whispers to no one that he is still around
watching his young and wife weep.

it will take 49 days of praying to send
him from this world into a parallel universe

above or beside the one felt on our faces.
his first-born will abstain from

the skin of animals until then, as the ancient monk
draped in deep orange counsels.

they leave the incense burning
drifting toward the biggest hole in the sky—

now they must search his overflowing closet
for burial clothes.

they will cut out the pockets
for the next life.

MARK LIPMAN
The Price of Doing Business

ATTENTION, Walmart Shoppers:

Somewhere …
… in the swollen bowels
of some dank and dimly lit
offshore sweatshop …

maybe in China, or Vietnam, or Bangladesh …
the lights are being turned out
in a young girl's eyes …

as she frantically stitches
her childhood away
one 12-hour shift at a time …

without sunlight
or bathroom breaks
or a proper education …

for pennies a day.

It's just Good Business.

It helps the bottom line,
when there are no labor laws,
or health requirements,
or pesky regulations
to get in the way
of the profits.

Make sure you take advantage
of our 3 for 1 special today.

We've got Congressmen for sale on aisle six
and we do accept food stamps
but unions are strictly forbidden.

We can't let little things
like human rights
and national sovereignty
stand in the way of progress,
stand in the way of the corporation
being able to freely trade
your life away
for dirt.

There are cargo ships on the horizon
and dividends to be paid.

So don't you worry about that fire,
or the factory that just collapsed
or that little girl turned to ash ...

that's just the price of doing business ...
and we always guarantee the lowest prices ...
because, we love ... our customers.

JAIME LOPEZ

Love Me, Rain

I feel it coming,
The clouds, the wind,
But the mystery,
When does it begin?

The pressure drops,
The blue turns gray,
Light turns to dark,
The tree branches sway.

I've ached for you,
Breathing through the dust,
I prayed for your return,
Gave it all my trust.

I hear you now,
Drumbeat touching all,
I want most to rise,
Only you, do I want to fall.

Your rhythm grows strong,
A song of serene,
Brown haze over me,
Is washed away clean.

You awaken my skin,
From my head down to my feet,
I'll drink *wherever* you land,
Wood, dirt, even concrete.

Don't leave me, my love,
I need your billion kisses,
Your blanket is life,
Your embrace never misses.

ROBERT MÄDER-KAMMER
Mom's War Stories

Albert, said his mom, was drafted at seventeen.
Many girls from poor families wore army Red Cross pins,
a red cross with a black broken cross.

Mom, sixteen, a conscript, with four weeks
of first aid got her new army Red Cross pin,
a pin with a black broken cross.

Albert's mom and my mom,
two twenty-something combat veterans,
sharing American coffee and American cigarettes,
cooking dinner together, sharing stories
of survival—the war stories only survivors can tell.

Mom said a grazing bullet caused the scar
on her forehead; caused by searching
for almost alive soldiers.
Albert's mom and my mom whisper,
I only understand a few words:
"men, soldiers, Russians, Germans,
and Americans."
I play by their feet,
resurrecting my toys
for another battle
under the kitchen table.

KARINEH MAHDESSIAN

Here

He has traveled far
To arrive with packed dreams and two babies
Here
He breaks his knees
Bends his back
Callouses his hands
And suns his cheeks
So his babies can eat, grow, play
He swallows his tongue
He cleans toilets and handles bullshit
He tears his flesh
He inhales dust
He coughs up blood
He is less than the man he imagined to be
He is hired feet
He does not know pleasure
His life is meant to be worked
He does not see doctors
There is no retirement
He will work
Until he is bones
He has nothing but his hands and his babies

KARINEH MAHDESSIAN

Return

Like ocean waves pulled by gravity
I return to myself
Shy
Awkward
And certainly too insecure
I giggle
Sashay hips
Mask hurt and anger
Into friendly gestures
I am more than the sum of my lovers
More than the angry slaps and ugly words
Hurled upon my body
I am more than one-night stand
Spread-eagle legs and wandering hands
I return to myself
Seeking refuge beneath strangers' bodies
The heat of their stench
I return to myself
Hide inside cocoons
Next time
I will be beautiful
Even if it is temporary
Let rain cleanse stains of sorrow from memory
43 beating hearts vanished into the dense of black
Where are my brothers?
Who steals their screams?
When does mourning begin?
Graveyards full of shadows taunt me
Yesterday they are gone.
Today they are gone.
Tomorrow they are gone.
How does sun shine
When stars are missing?

RUTHIE MARLENÉE
Christmas in Duarte

His homies called him Christmas
for the gifts he scored and poured
from his bag of tricks,
for the rock candy and snowballs
he stuffed into stockings
with a twinkle in his eyes
and a smile to light up the skies of Duarte.

Christmas was marked.
He knew he'd never see 17,
but dared to believe in change.
Not much older than Jesus,
he entered the Temple to chase
away the money mongers,
those defilers of his hood.

No more dope, no more waste.
He toyed with the idea of hope;
rubbed its sweetness across his gums,
Black vs. brown, naughty or nice;
His homies might like a taste.
Hope wouldn't cost the price
of a lung, a tattooed arm or a leg;

He turned his back. I'd like to think
he was headed home
before the five shots rang out,
ripping metal through flesh,
shattering bone,
piercing his heart.

Christmas is over.
His blood turns to rust
on the sidewalk
where wide-eyed Teddy bears' dreams die;
where penny candles burn out and poinsettias lie, wilting;
where Santa's milk curdles; and
where Mama's cookies crumble to dust.

RUTHIE MARLENÉE
Cuate, the Barrio Drunk

I watched the wounded, weathered warrior
push a shopping cart—or was it pulling him
over train tracks across asphalt searing
holes through the soles of his *zapatos*
as he shuffled past the smoldering
shell of a Chevy on his way to sell soda
and beer bottles to the shops up on Central.

I got too close when I offered him
my daddy's empties. He smelled
like pee and something familiar
like Thunderbird and sadness.
His name was *Cuate* [coo-ah'tay]
because he used to be a twin until
his brother got killed in Korea.

He had no other family and took
shelter in the stinky sewer tunnel
under the tremorous train tracks.
I watched him raise an arm shielding
himself from the kids who laughed,
throwing stones like grenades.
He cursed, *pinche cabrones*, and he bled,

as he trudged and tramped up to the Safeway.
There was nothing I could do to stop them
or to save him. He was on a mission
to deliver the dead soldiers of the barrio
and once rewarded for those bottles,
with his wounds licked, and rations stocked,
Cuate would journey back to the frontlines.

JEFFERY MARTIN

The Poverty of Access

It cheats a long line of tired, withered hands
coursing through generation after generation
of veins too weary to imagine
a kinder existence

It cheats brilliant minds
it cheats brilliant minds
it cheats brilliant minds
leaving them suffocating on a frustration
they can no longer define

It cheats limber bodies
that have no idea
they were meant to dance

dance in the four directions of life
meshing with the deities of
wind fire earth and water
creating light bright
and transforming

The poverty of access
closes books before sentences are complete
before action can coincide with thought
before the mind body and spirit
introduce themselves

This poverty is harshest amongst its young
for it starves them intellectually
long before ravaging their stomachs

It says no you can't and means it
it says you are unworthy

and means it
it says here is where you belong
and means it

The poverty of access
steals souls as well as land
murders ambition as well as men and women
who ask too many questions
it fills prisons and dungeons
with corpses breathing yet
breathless

moving yet motionless
eating yet starved

It gives prostitution its place
then sneers
it gives violence its place
then sneers
it gives homelessness its place
then sneers
it gives crime its place
and then claims prophecy

This poverty of access
does not tell stories
it stunts them

with nasty words like
cannot
will not
must not

It is a poverty that guarantees
an outcome as unfair
as it is unwarranted

RUBÉN MARTÍNEZ

"Contrabando y traición":
A Critical Karaoke

We begin on the border
The one she must cross to live
Even if her body might snag on the fence

It is 1974 and Homeland Security
Is still a generation away
But the New Jim Crow emerges
With Nixon's War on Drugs
Legislative big business rubberstamped
Ever since by Democrats and Republicans alike

It is 1974 and I am 12 years old
In San Salvador at *el Club Deportivo*
I'm listening to "Band on the Run"
As I sip my first-ever *Cuba Libre*

While *Los Tigres del Norte* live in San Jose
Having arrived as teenagers
Looking for a break in the Alta California sun

Two years later I'll hit on my first joint
Four years after that my first bump of blow
Both of which crossed the line
With couriers smooth-talking their way
Past the moustache-belly *migras*
At the San Clemente checkpoint

Ah, *el corrido*! Keeping it real
Since *la Revolución*—
Characters, caricatures drawn finely as Posada
From the streets to the song from the song
To the myth, gods walking among us

Let's imagine Emilio Varela, *jefe* of the operation
In polyester and aviators
And his accomplice, Camelia
La Tejana, Chicana from San Antonio
In denim and choker
He betrays her, all the convincing she needs
In a few seconds he'll be dead by lead
And she'll squeal away on eight cylinders

This is the foundational *narco-corrido*
The newscast of the rural poor
On the *ranchos* with their *tres animalitos*
Perico, gallo, y chiva
I consumed all three in L.A.
Even as I reported on the crack wars
Connected to the civil war
In my mother's El Salvador
Land of poets and guerrillas
Who today play incumbents
Against insurgent *narco-maras*

Forty years later
Camelia and Emilio are quaint
Folk heroes of a bygone era
Me, I'm more or less clean
But there's blood on my hands
From the student in Ayotzinapa
Lying in the street faceless
Not because he doesn't have a name
—He is, was, Julio César,
19 years old, first year student
At *Escuela Normal Rural Raúl Isidro Burgos*—
But because the cops the *narcos* the *politicos*
On both sides of the border
Literally peeled off his face
You can Google the image
All the darkness that fingers us
Is at our fingertips

Today there is no Chapo Robin Hood Guzmán
And there is no border separating the blood
Spilled there from the mourning here
The overdose here and the impunity there
In the virtual ether there are permanent links
To faceless body-*víctimas*
Whose names we must revere
With silence

Silence the only way to face
        What is unspeakable
Silence the only way to do
        No more harm with language
Silence the only way to make what was profaned
        Sacred again

Por los 43 y demás normalistas de Ayotzinapa
Por los migrantes centroamericanos que se encontraron con
        La Bestia en el camino
Por la poeta Susana Chávez de Juárez quien dijo
        "Ni una muerta más," para convertirse en una más

For the dismembered and the un-remembered
For the landscape brushed with blood
For the body receiving blows in low resolution video

Por el hombro con el tatuaje de una cometa
Por la que ya no pronuncia el Rosario
Por el desierto testigo de todo

For the overdose
For the prison time
For the body that needs a name

Pido silencio
I ask for silence

February 14

It is St. Valentine's Day, and
the room is full of musical balloons.
My students throw paper clips at one which plays
How Sweet It Is (To Be Loved By You) above my head.
Everywhere are flowers:
orange, white, lavender.
All my students carry them
and we pause in our studies
to read love poems in French,
write more in English,
Spanish, all the languages.
The L.A. Times wants to eliminate Valentine's Day,
but I declare every day St. Valentine's Day!
We will fill the elevators with roses;
we will hug each other at random and without reservation;
we will demand unconditional affection from strangers,
and we will not stop until
we are running down the halls yelling,
"I love you more than sardines,
more than leafy sea dragons,
more than green tea leaves!"
"I love you more than cedar wood,
more than gel pens, more than prayer flags!"

RHIANNON MCGAVIN
"L'Heritage"

My mother says, bloom where you are planted
and French canals kept her watered
She colors my eyes as parisian rain
She tells me of the southern sands,
with beach umbrellas like the candies she'd bring back in pink tins
She would tuck me in at night with borrowed maps,
whispering that we were here, in the barges and bakeries
She did not say that we are also in the soil and air
She feeds me *quiche l'oignon* but I grew most
on the longing for my grandmother's village,
le village de la mére de sa mére de sa mére encore
I have never seen my mother's France, of mossy sidewalks and blessed memory
or the town she thinks was ours, before the first brick was laid for Auschwitz
She has to show me postcards instead of family pictures
I am always too young to hear of the murders
but mom swears my bones are strong as rock
and I know that every step I take is in mourning
être juive to be Jewish is to be born during a funeral
Flowers do not garnish the graves, they are for the living,
they don't grow fast enough
but there will always be more stones to stack in the cemetery,
by a school, a bleeding kosher market—
I am always nine hours behind translating the headlines
I am so tired of counting, *un* dead, *trois* dead, *quatre* dead
I am tired of conjugating, *courir* (to run), *tuer* (to kill)
but everything sounds beautiful *en française, non?*
Even the slurs have a crystal echo
although I do not care for the dagger that follows
je veux fleurir comme la rose de l'ete
Maman I want to bloom like a summer rose
Ima save me from being cut like Toulouse and Marseilles
and Paris and Paris and Paris
because I know that we too belong here,

in our Friday dinners and perfume
but the catacombs are seething
Maman tell me again about my grandmother's grandfather,
le grand rabbi du Paris
Do not think of how he would fall, learning that in January,
his synagogue closed on Shabbat for the first time since the German
    occupation
Ima tell me about the stained glass windows, in so many more colors than red.
I tell her, we are still going home
No ash could ever keep us
but this is our life now, watching the white roses
my Nana planted pull scarlet from the earth
It comes in drops and streaks, how deep their roots must reach
When I was younger, I would lick rainwater off the petals and think,
this is what love tastes like
Now I know that it is the salt on your lips,
with a lullaby so soft, the metal can't find you

ELENA MINOR

Historia de un amor

They lie and they believe it—old *cuentos* told and retold: the pull of legend holds strong. '*Pos*, that's the way it happened, *mano. Así mero pasó*,' they say time and time again. '*¿Y sabes qué más …?* and add their part.

Sooner or sometimes later they mostly all die and become that very told tale. They blast each other open & shut, or someone shivs them and criss-cuts their organs as if gutting a pig, or bashes in their skulls until their brains splat out to lie in the thick juice of their own cooling blood, there to stew then curdle for *mosca* food and when done, be served up as *pura leyenda*, prized story, love of remembrance, all loves passed: soul possession.

Then sooner or sometimes later, some sad shadow steps out, offers it up on a platter, with peppered dressing, on the side. *Drink them bones, ey. Sup on gamey, ungarnished flesh.*

Becomes famous and makes a rep. Maybe even hawks the show on the road, *aquí y allá* (*por esos rumbos extranjeros*). Recites a little, but when asked aside tells a slightly different story.

It's that lessons learned serve art—his—hers—theirs—ours: to open mic as it closes in / to out, goes down for applause and then, it's on to read au-tographs, or sign obituaries. Drink black coffee. Net the night. Surrender.

ELENA MINOR

Singer, Not Song

Since finding the last word on
sale and snatching it right up
I have been greedy—a hoarder
of dreams and what-ifs

I watch this word vigilantly
Never let it out of my reach
Take it with me wherever I go—
[tuck it carefully in the far left

front most compartment of my purse—
within easy reach—cheek to jowl
with my iPhone next to my cash wallet
ID and credit cards]

I don't let anyone know I have it
Lest they try to take it from me
Rise it to the Cloud
Cache it for their own selfish purposes—

use it in ways I never will and
in my living room I've built a shrine
for it—a beggar's *ofrenda*
with imagined marigolds

dried *pan dulce* chocolate and under the rose
petals a faded old *foto-*
graphic of that poem I never had
to write

PENELOPE MOFFET

Cutlery

"MEEK LITTLE WIVES FEEL THE EDGE OF THE CARVING KNIFE AND STUDY
THEIR HUSBANDS' NECKS."
—RAYMOND CHANDLER, "RED WIND"

The forks ran away with the spoons
and ended up suspended
by fishing line
beneath an inverted eggcup
hung at the lip
of my third-story nest,
still when the air is still,
chiming sweetly
when a breeze
pushes through needled boughs,
pinecones puffing
tangerine dust
on cacti and orchids
tipped toward the sun.

Faint silvery song,
gentle even when
fierce Santa Ana winds
make music out of cutlery.

There are no knives
among these spoons,
and forks are clumsy tools
for cutting, even
when they're not
suspended in mid-air.
Orange pollen
on the balcony rail
is just dirt
where earth

is chained by concrete.
It's good that we're apart.
I can give you so much
and no more, no more
of my heart.

BILL MOHR

Real Days Off

Since when is not
every day accounted for?
Suppose one is lucky
enough to have first
pick of days off
so that you can claim
the Thursday and Friday
before Independence Day,
and since it falls on
a Monday, and
this job has weekends
off, you get a five
day vacation using
only two of your
allotment. Thursday
is for laundry
and your eye
appointment
and Friday
for the brake job
on your 15 year
old car. Three
days left until
the abyss
beckons.
A few hours
with a beach umbrella
on Sunday will
suffice for a
survival memory.

BILL MOHR

Complexities

A bag of oranges
doesn't appear
to be heavy
but hold one
yourself and count
three hundred
cars driving by.
As she stands between
the stack of salty
peanuts and dusty
grapes, the bag
gets heavier and it
retains that heaviness
when it's passed through
the window; and the driver,
hoisting it onto
the passenger's seat,
thinks, this is a lot of
fruit for two dollars.

Border Crossing

I stop and look North and South and look where I may go.
Receive open arms and I hug my lonely Los Angeles;
I nurse you with my sweat.
Speaking Spanish rescues me sometimes from your jaws.
It gives me a sense of direction.
But it does not give me financial freedom.
So I stop and start turning without direction
While I speak Spanish and English.

I get strength by longing about our history
And about my goal-oriented spirit.
I pronounce my name and the sound travels
Through the street dragging my images all the way down
Until my name is a shout sliding between buildings.

When my name returns as I start thinking, and
Thinking, speeding and speeding, thinking, and speeding,
I build my strategic plan.
Plan my certainty.
Plan to make a blockbuster.
Plan to see us, the hybrid men saving the world
And plan to enforce my bilingual power.

I am starting to advance.
Puedo hacer esto y lo otro.
I can dress Latin and French words
So they stay in my head,
And I can conquer English illiteracy.

I tell my fellow Latinos who work as cashiers at the grocery store
That I am not speaking English to forget my culture:
Yo soy su brother; hermano, vine de allá… también.
I would never leave my people behind.

However, if I don't speak English,
I will be left behind.
And will continue halting, and turning
In the core of the city   In the core of history
In the core of sophistication.
Necessary, not for sport, but obligation.
Economical obligation   Cultural obligation
And linguistic obligation.

We will be left behind
Atrás quedará la bola;

Nothing works if I stay on the border.

Boiling Rice

My mother still wants to cook for my father,
but she doesn't remember.
When she leaves the kitchen to watch TV,

when she leaves the living room
to grab her sweater, when she walks out
to the patio to sit with the dog
until the rice stops boiling,
and burns, that's when my father tells her,
Amor, please, no more cooking.

The next morning he finds a plate
of steaks thawing in the cupboard.
Then he prepares her breakfast
of cereal and coffee
while she rocks at the table,
the same meal every morning,
the same shock of wild gray hair.

She erupts with
I need to go shopping with Victoria—
my mother doesn't remember
that her sister died two years ago.

After breakfast, my mother sits
on the Paul Bunyan bench in the patio,
only her toes whisk the bricks
and when she leans back,
her feet hang in the breeze.

SYBIL MOSELY

A Clamor

A clamoring party of birds outside is urging me to
shake off distorted moods.

They know that warm and deceitful sensations
Of waking under a caul will not
Be adequate defense of my weightless dreams.

The birds keep raising riot.
By their congress, against the misty sky of morning
My tree is claimed.

MAJID NAFICY

Promenade at Dawn

The cobblestones are soaked with the scent of passersby
The coffee shops are watching with heavy eyelids
The empty benches are listening to each other
The black phone handsets are waiting for caressing hands
And a yellow fire hydrant
Is crouching like a mystic.

I stop by Midnight Special Bookstore
And smile at Charles Baudelaire
Who has come to the edge of our early morning city
From the depths of his Parisian night,
To touch the sun on this shiny window.
Ah!
Here, not Paris,
But my little Promenade yawns.

The Russian musicians
Do not circle with their muzhik boots
And a Chinese chime player
Does not chant at his chapel
And six Indian dancers
Do not whirl around with their drums and flutes
And my little son
Does not look shyly at
A Beethoven-playing girl.

I like this full emptiness
And as I empty my pockets
From last night's left-over notes
I whistle to the hungry doves.

MAJID NAFICY

Santa Monica Farmers' Market

I hear this dialect
With its silent "J"
Singing everywhere.
It is Wednesday's market
Near Santa Monica beach
With the scent of Persian basil
Chinese sugar peas
and Mexican *jalapeños*.
A woman smiles at me
Behind the jars of honey.
Flowers have covered her muumuu
And "B"s are buzzing in her words.
I walk over the bridge
Looking at the cars below,
Passing, oblivious to me.
I know, on Freeways
All signs are written in English.
But my sorrow knows only Persian.

JANET NIPPELL

L.A. Rockabye

New baby not yet called by your name,
I nursed and tiptoed you to the crib.
I swayed on my feet, a rooted swaying,
until I felt you fold into sleep.

After we kids were too big to be held
we labored up a cedar tree
on red scaly branches fit to our grips—
rungs sprung so densely out of the trunk
we had to shinny pointing our toes so as
not to rake trailing tennis shoes off.

With our grandparents' shingles below,
the sidewalk almost too far down to look,
we dangled our legs off worn level boards
our father had dragged up so long before
bark flowed around their edges in folds.
When the wind blew, what lank mystery—

but down came the cedar, seat boards and all,
before you were born. We drove by to see
the old house knocked into apartment buildings.
I lower you swaddled to your crib bed—
will you run out to a tangle, sharp scented,
will you find such a sanctuary?

HARRY E. NORTHUP
Young Latina Writes in Her Journal

"Maybe she just loves to write,"
my wife said.
"Maybe it's the one peaceful place
she has," I replied.
We each said yes to each other.

It was the second evening I had
seen this young Latina.
Last evening, she had rested her
journal on a flat part of an open
gate to courtyard apartments
& was writing. This evening,
she was sitting on the 4' high
platform. Her skirt was pulled up
& she was writing in her journal.

About 10 minutes before I passed
her I was walking east on Sunset.
I was thinking about narcissism.
Make a list of things that are
the opposite: Altruism; helping
others; thinking about others;
being considerate about others;
be curious of others; listen to
others' interests; to be the others
in a room—to not be the only one
in a room with others.

A friend of mine said. I listened.

"Maybe she's doing an assignment
from high school: writing about what
she sees on her street in the evening."

"Maybe she just likes to write."

HARRY E. NORTHUP

East Hollywood 3

mariposa avenue

"do you like kobe?"
"named my son after him"

"i love kobe"
"me, too,
everybody do"

korean postal clerk

"my daughter tells me
i am over the hill.
i tell her i am a sunset."

mariposa avenue

the woman in brown wears
perfume as she waters the lawn

MARTIN OTT
Caves of Los Angeles

There was once a valley and parched
land that gulped water and settlers,

underground aqueducts for manna
rays and merfolk crooning chanteys

beneath asphalt, drawing legions
to explore the uncharted depths.

Bubble up in mouth froth and dew,
beneath condor wings, airplane fumes.

There was once a weary traveler,
who settled at a wine bar, noticing

a woman in a wedding dress and combat
boots, dark eyeliner and tear tattoos.

He was fixated on her chest where hung
a murky blue broach the color of L.A.

sky, and discovered that she had not
opened it for fear of finding herself.

She let him fumble with the clasp
in her bedroom covered with a carpet

of clothes and unpaid bills to feel
for the thin layer hidden there.

Rise to melodies of coffin and egg,
lost things and unanswered rings.

There was once an unemployed man about
to lose his home in North Hollywood,

and he agreed to let a studio rip up
his garage foundation to bury body

parts for a small sum, for a film
about an actor turned serial killer.

Plastic bone pieces were painted
by art school grads, wrapped in duct

tape strips and red tar. He saw hands
stained in the business of the buried,
even make-believe, but this opened
hole and rubble, this wound, was real.

Don't narrow the aperture to dusk.
Knock on air, and let yourself in.

MARTIN OTT

California is Sinking

It was water draining, earthquakes kissing in the shade of the moon
winking in tune with the marionettes of Godzilla tap dancing for dinner.
It was the office pool being rigged before the steering column in the ribs,
the storage shed turned into a homeless brig, the matador's cape or baby's
bib hung in the closet or on a billboard begging for consideration, the fib
that became the real story rehashed until time lost its will. It was the small
screen sucking us in, the vodka gimlet transformed into gin, the famed
taco truck up in smoke that we followed for years, the treasure in limbo
just beyond the beyond, the yolk discarded in the heart-smart omelet.
It was the drone sent out for cigarettes by the director lost in the desert.
It was the lost scene in Steinbeck's last work. It was the invisible collapse
of the land's face, stretched taut like an actor turned professional patient.
It was the hidden reservoir beneath the migrants streaming into the void.
It was the crash that no one heard and the warnings we pretended to ignore.

MELINDA PALACIO
Broken Bone Poem

Bird houses follow me to the emergency room. Earlier,
turquoise wedges betray me, catch on emerald stairs,
fibula snaps in two and my ankle dislocates ugly.

Time to pay a debt to a gypsy curse,
says my grandmother.

We have wide, chubby, infallible feet.
Watch out for our twirls and tall strides.
Taut calf muscles offer a salute to any onlooker.

But somewhere along the line, a curse.
My grandmother has fallen all over Europe.
She fell flat on her face in her own kitchen.

I've taken a spill or two, missed a curb in tennis shoes.
Once I fell in three-inch black patent heels.
But, oh, I cannot blame my shoes.

How I tumbled like Humpty Dumpty,
followed a white rabbit into a wonderland
called morphine, ketamine, percocet, oxycodone.

Bone healers put me back together,
sewed equal pieces of my flesh into one.
In my recurring nightmare, I spiral into an abyss.

What part of gravity do I not understand or
why doesn't gravity understand me?

How to break the curse that caused quick lightning pain,
the snap of bone and a wrong-facing foot?
A substantial body becomes bird-like and free.

Lying down on the floor of our green Honda, I see treetops.
Bird houses, tall balconies, and a widow's walk.
No ghost, my bird's eye view begs mercy.

Before surgery, the daintiest bird house, painted pink and yellow, greets me.
White porch, white picket fence, and white lace doily around the base,
a pretty distraction for a broken foot.

RAE PARIS

Uncle Kwanza: November 1

This isn't a photograph but it might as well be the way it's framed
in my head, the first time we journey to New Orleans.

You let us empty pennies from glass jars as tall as our small bodies,
thousands from glass jars now rows of urns against the wall.

We, my sisters and I, sit and count one, two, three, four, all the way up
to fifty, stuffing faded paper rolls with your found treasure.

In the background of this photo that isn't, you laugh, call my father
Bubba, the brother he was before he escaped to L.A.

You were already Muslim, *first fruit of the harvest*, a name you claimed
your own self, shedding Milton to some faux paradise.

In the counting, we blame each other for making us lose our place, and I
wonder if you're rich, all these pennies, so much for my young hands.

I think only someone who gathers money he might never count must
know something about love, wanting, or end of days.

And I wanted to know things like why I sensed my father's fear returning
to the place that made him, or what words to ask about this ache.

No one knows how you made it from the Casino to Emergency, but
let's say you won big, let's say your pockets were filled with silver.

Let's not think about your blocked heart, broken, let's say you felt the meaning
of your name, new bounty, as free as any man, Black, can feel.

Tell Bubba hello, tell him I don't know what to do with the space he
used to take up, but say I'm figuring it out, tell him.

Remove the coins from your dead eyes, remove our eyes give them our dead, to
remove our dead give them our only eyes, maybe, maybe…

Maybe I'll walk to the river, toss some pennies, maybe let's wish some-
thing first and full remove our dead eyes fruit for all of us.

CANDACE PEARSON

From the Permanent Collection

SELF-PORTRAIT WITH OIL DERRICK, PERSISTENT

Here the artist has chosen a classic gesture—
up, down, down, up, to portray determination,
a certain doggedness. This is a subject willing to do

the dirty work, to clean up after others' more
dramatic messes. Loyal, fixed-gaze. Stalwart. Is this
too much praise for such a conventional choice?

> *I bow to the Miocene wing and bone,*
> *tusk and claw and shell. Deep to the sludge,*
> *to the warming core.*

Bobbing without weaving.
Never sideways; sideways is suspicious,
you know, a deviation.

> *Search out the viscous matter*
> *hidden in pockets of shale and shard.*

Wait, did you miss it, there in the upper corner?
The hesitation, the pause.

CANDACE PEARSON

From the Permanent Collection

SELF-PORTRAIT WITH ROADSIDE GRAVE MARKER

First, consider the composition: middle quadrant
dominated by simple pine cross, white paint already
transmogrifying, faith bleached and pocked.

In the foreground, plastic roses, picked at by crows,
color bled by July sun.

Note the depth of field—crossbeams spill shadows
on untilled ground. And in the background, blurred
by the lens: an orchard, late fruit shriveled.

> *I am the remembered and the one who remembers.*
> *I am the cross, I am the shifting soil.*
> *Holder of effigies and altars.*
> *The note that releases its alphabet to the air.*

The name has faded, I think it begins with a C or T.
We may never see it clearly.

ALICE PERO

Word Hummingbirds

The children dip and hover over the words,
not sure if they are hawks or hummingbirds

A dollar sign stymies one little girl
Perhaps in her world, there has only been an absence of them,
a hollow hole of few dollars
So few that the sign shrank away from the paper
like a frightened syllable

Words dance in the children's mouths
They throw words across the room to one another,
unafraid of collisions and explosions,
laughing at the sight and sound of phrases that split and splatter,
all colors of the rainbow
They beg to make more, as though words were pancakes
covered with syrup, precious sweet things they can eat

Skipping through them and jumping over them, but never landing,
reading, reading, reading, they leap and push ahead, not knowing meanings
"Three Musketeers," "grim," "radio wave,"
Guessing and stumbling, plunging in the half-dark, no one there to explain,
Explicame, no tiene sentido

Flying blind, like vibrating bats, radar is all they have,
even if pretending, they will find the way

ALICE PERO

Desert Hot Springs

They say the water here is magic
If your man is killed in battle
you come to these springs
Wash your face and hair
blessed with pure water spirit

Those who drink these waters
live long in wisdom
Those who breathe the sacred winds
learn to soar with them

Now the German-born ladies arrive
from Vancouver, Oregon, Chicago,
stay for a month or two
soak their arthritic bones
in the clear, warm water

They drink coffee and chatter
in their native tongue at poolside
as wild breezes try to tease
their napkins away

The Swiss flag flying over this tidy spa
looks like a Red Cross flag
No one notices or comments

Here windows and tile can hold no dirt
The spotless Mexican maid scrubs
and the wind takes care of the rest
Walls and floors gleam
smiling in perpetual sun

When death comes
wind and sand will blow it away
as it keeps pesky bees off sparkling
dinner plates

RAMONA PILAR

Six Lines to Thirty Eight

Mom and me. Mom and he.
Never had a 15; *Treintañera, ¡sí!*
Bachelor and Mistress: my degrees.
Pallbearer princess carried her dad. *Adios.*
Soy chula y sola. ¡Dime hola!
Nor Cal; So Cal: All me.

colors i have been

ignorant, unknowing white
despairing obsidian
golden playful enchanted
sensual scarlet
cerulean sky visionary
storm sea struggle
blushing wisteria love
crimson throbbing ache
verdant emerald becoming
burnt clay orange shame
translucent poem
midnight starscape wonder
brave unflinching indigo
smashed tomato fury
canary bliss
passionate purple
azure consciousness

HOLLY PRADO

Pursuit of Happiness

Our last name was full of cousins. My first name: no one
got to be Holly but me. Family blood, human imagination.

Walt Whitman's "multitudes."
Adrienne Rich's "dream of a common language."

Yes, America's insistence on the singular—one strong hand
reaching for your arm: Diane Wakoski: "And I remember that part
of the evening better than anything else..." Beckian Fritz Goldberg:
"I thought as a girl/it was not my war." Harry Northup:
"Nebraska, where I threw baseball after baseball..."

Every poet moves every pen, but nobody says what I can say.
Our poetry is Beowulf translated by Tu Fu translated by
Amiri Baraka translated by me. There's no poem without

urgent longing for each other; no language without my desperation
for the woman only I'd become, years away from my whole family's
dark suspicions about dreamers. Step into the vigorously familiar,

dear and unsuspecting reader, the slide into the blind and hungry,
open-mouthed unknown. This is America:
Your own hand on my trembling arm.

HOLLY PRADO

I Need the Sanctified. I Need the Obvious

Groceries in their sturdy bags:
one day's difficulty, matched with kindness—
young man who loads my groceries in the car
says he's off early, needs to be with his niece
and nephew because his sister has to work.

In the grocery store, I stopped to read the label on lozenges
for my husband's cold. I got in someone's way, apologized.
She said, "We need to read those labels carefully." She meant
this seriously. So do I, sympathizing with the uncle, young,
who has a job and then his other job of family. Colds mend,

eventually. Little children struggle, but they do grow up to be ourselves,
to have long patience with our labels, names of the ingredients
and when to put those in our mouths.

It's work to be a sister with two kids. It's work to be
my husband with a January cold—coughing, weary.
It's work to be a child. We work at what we are.
Later in the day, it helps when I can hear a story with
more story and more story—then the resolution, all this
from a friend who sits beside me, showing me the words
she writes for family, self, and dying. Resolution:

kindness given to my groceries, packed as neatly as the gifts
I guess they are—gifts for how we cook and eat, how Kleenex
helps a stuffy nose, how writing brings the whole grand, tiny
world that fits around me to its heart. Strangers, husband, friend.
The woman's comment about things we hope will heal:
Read carefully. Read every single word.

ARTURO QUIROS
Gasoline Dreams

In the boiling heat of Belize
My father cut sugar cane like an African slave
Restrained by chains
Short-changed dollar amounts
Because my grandfather
He couldn't count
The tropical breeze brought a brief relief
His Indian skin burning like a Vietnamese monk
Protesting in Saigon
Swallowed by flames
Unveiling the truth
Today I pour gasoline from the oil fields of Iraq
Onto this blaze of bones I once called home
I protest in peace to combat those who lack the facts
Photograph the past with words
This pen my only weapon
I blast back like John Trudell
From the banks of hell
Every time I see Columbus sail
I'm a conscientious objector
A militant messenger
Trying to find a way
To escape this poverty-infested landscape
Deserted on the outskirts by those who gave birth
To the American dream
The murderous money schemes
That tried to kill my culture
And fed dead soldiers patriotic garbage
I'm a demonstrator of something greater
An obvious target for those who fear change
But I'm not here to win or rearrange borders
Where my brothers and sisters die daily
I'm a witness dreaming a new world into being

Seeing beyond the surface
One deep breath at a time
As bombs continue to fall from beautiful skies.

A. RAZOR

If Bubba's Taxi Could Talk

This city, like all cities, is changing
I'm rolling along, changing too

The days seem different now, as I
come & go, the faces greet themselves
never me

But, I don't mind so much
I'm just looking for work
in an über world religion
that cashed out long ago

There is just gizmos galore
A button to push for everyone
A button to come & a button to go

They say unemployment is low
That's why I don't collect it
Don't want to fuck w/ the numbers
Might put folks in a panic

I'm eyeballing what I got left
to call my own
               thinking about
what fits into a
               100lb backpack
while I can
still carry such a load
with the ease of a ballerina
dancing in the dilapidated opera house
as the fire that we set together
begins to lick up into the rafters

& the building shudders & shivers

before she begins to drop flaming
pieces down on us from above

& the music is our heartbeats
& the music is our screaming

No ladies, fat or thin, left to carry a tune
just flat tires on all the wheels that
haven't come off already, just one last

twirl, & my ballerina act is done

Just a 100lb pack for what I got left
& then maybe a lil' music that has

yet to be prophesied right here

ELLEN REICH

After the Rape

after he parks his navy-blue van
     and enters the hiking path
after he lures the female jogger deep into the woods
     on the pretext that a baby deer is wounded
after he laughs in her face
     when she discovers the lie
after he pulls out a knife saying he needs to slice her neck
     just enough to make her pass out
after he slits her nylon shorts
     and her rayon underpants
after he removes her sweat-socks and running shoes
     she revives in time for his plunge into her
after he rapes she runs wild through the woods
     and out to the street, incoherent and nude
after I calm her she repeats
     I was so stupid
after a car passes and the driver hands her an army blanket
     to cover herself, she sits on the curb
after she tells me her children are at the campsite
     I run past cabin after cabin, closed for the off-season
after I find an open door I phone for help and the officers
     meet me in the middle of the road
after I take them to her where people have begun to gather and stare
     the detective stays until dark questioning her
after that, every male driver of every navy-blue van
     is the rapist

STEVEN REIGNS
Morning, West Hollywood

The sun rises at 6:16 a.m.
moves morning along La Brea Boulevard
overtaking last night's marquee lights at the Gateway,
past the Formosa Café where the ghosts
of Douglas Fairbanks and Mary Pickford still dine.

Day moves west to where Russian Jews settled
en masse to escape Nazism and Fascism,
when Hollywood didn't offer complete freedom.
Light arcs over bakeries and grocers
selling *babka*, bagels, *baba ghanoush*.
Signs reveal another alphabet,
a melting pot of generations and cultures.

Then sunrise finds The Sunset Strip,
the reverberation still sounding
from rock concerts and nightclubs,
glimmers off the blue pole billboard.

At Plummer Park, old men will play chess
to pass the day. Residents recall the beginning
of the plague before AIDS Project Los Angeles and Being Alive
stepped in to offer healing and hope.

At Westbourne Drive, a rainbow flag catches
the morning breeze, flaps alongside
symbols for our city and state.
At San Vicente, brightly colored crosswalks
remind with every step that diversity matters,
isn't just tolerated but is honored.

The sun warms the library, the Design Centers,
the Recovery Center, the Melrose galleries, and the Troubadour

where Joni, Janis, and James all played.
Sun moves past Doheny toward the Pacific.

Everyday we wake up, a brilliant and creative people
in a beautiful city, our past and present
intersecting, illuminated, full of promise
and possibility.

LUIVETTE RESTO
Fingerprints on Tortilla

Before mouths agape into a yawn
and eyes squint at the sun's strength

Cielo mixes the *masa harina con agua*
rolling them evenly into twelve balls

petite, five inch hands pressing them flatter
than any tortilla maker sold in the *marquetas*

after that—
it was the silent relationship
between her fingers and the *comal*.

> *How come she never winced or said* hijo'le *when she flipped them?*

Her culinary talents
preceded her at U.S. Citizenship and Immigration Services

> *We can't get a clear fingerprint, Mrs. Castro.*
> *They seemed to be burned off.*

Rubbing her fingers together
Cielo spoke about the *comal*
like a Borges novel.

How she tempered it
not by the numbers on the knobs
but by *ojo* like *bisabuela* Eulalia taught her
watching the tri-color flames hover over the gas grate
like the celestial glory prophesied in Bibles,
hugging the bottom of the cast iron
with its blue, purple, and white fingers.

This was her sunrise ritual
in satisfying six appetites
with refrigerated butter
con un poco de sal or eggs
wrapped
running after school buses.

Does this ruin my chances?

No, Mrs. Castro. We will find a way.
Let me try one more time.

LUIVETTE RESTO

The Kind of Woman

I never took you for the kind of woman
to let others sip her gin,
allowing the unacceptable to happen.

Letters address me: tough vixen
while *comadres* stand like sirens with songs that begin
I never took you for the kind of woman

echoing hymns born from the breath of the feminine
who never adhere to discipline.
Allowing the unacceptable to happen

underneath a transatlantic sky, widen
by a thousand moons, still like a mannequin.
I never took you for the kind of woman

who gave up searching for her own heroine
vibrant and memorable like tattoos on the skin,
allowing the unacceptable to happen.
Catholic verses brazen
and overlapping W's on the chest, remind with chagrin
I never took you for the kind of woman
allowing the unacceptable to happen.

ERIKA REYES

For My Best Friend

Growing up, we were two little monsters.
We would jump the fence,
We'd make slingshots,
We would even make the neighbor cry.

Growing up, yeah, we were two little girls.
We would play store
Count change,
Buy random objects.
The world was ours to own.

We wore smiles on our faces
And when the smiles were gone
A joke or two,

A push
A shove
Would rush it all back to fun.

I would like to think that the two of us
Are still playing,
Still running around in each other's mind,
When things get low
Because life gets tough.

I'd like to think that the goodbye letter
Written in Spanish
Is not all that's left
Of us

MICHAEL REYES
Math Quizzes at Breakfast

To be like my pops
you can't be photogenic.
Circa my twentieth birthday:
eyelids rolled shut, grinning
with polished, immaculate teeth
like collectible state quarters
of my childhood.
You have to read superhero fiction
to your boy at bedtime
and pronounce English words
like they cut your tongue.
Get yourself a towering truck, too,
that sighs when it gets home.
Math quizzes at breakfast
before school,
and afterwards,
because his pops did the same,
borderline à la mustached dictator.
You must order a bitter iced tea
and eyeball everyone's food
and wear fancy button-ups
with cargo shorts and running shoes,
sometimes a baseball cap.
You need to leave behind
fat tips, always,
because maybe the waiter
depends on it like rainwater
for the roots of sugarcane,
or the roots of his boy
from the Mexico photographs, a grin
but not so photogenic.

MICHAEL REYES
Atypical Love Poem

Our style is desolate, nameless taco truck for dates, fast food in
your silver Civic under streetlamps announcing old finger
scribbles on foggy windows.

I inhale my day, you exhale yours and palm your face because
insults live in my jokes' crevices like garbage I tuck in your side
door compartment to find later with a snark and forgiving smile.

We joke why we're together, sometimes believe it because we
know our past unlike we know our future:

fights in every part of the city, in your car against backdrops
of burning candle skyscrapers and garbaged, graffiti alleys with
cats as witnesses to some argument that makes no sense the next
day, but left a check mark knee scar that hurts when cold.

And sometimes I blame it on *this* self-diagnosis you say I entitle,
and my eyes slice at the words. Because I never learned to feel
and can't love you with a smile everyday.

I'm sorry it's me thinking against your chatterbox that *this* will
become a love poem one day. Our relationship is leave and
return like breath to a car window, or collide and see the bruise
later. It's push back car seats to make space for unfolding
ourselves into each other, forgoing stop signs.

And sometimes it feels some kind of ordinary, but our
relationship is pure black silence, interrupted with the screenlight
from text messages.

THELMA T. REYNA

Night Rituals

he keeps a bucket by his bed
filled with water for when nightmares come

for when he sees again his buddy's hand
dangling on a vein, legs pulped, entrails out

for when ash and redness trespass clouds,
smother throats and bring down birds like stones

for when he crawls in dust past rocks, arms,
severed heads, and humvees like upended bugs

for when nightmares wrestle him from bed,
back home, dozen years of duty done

on knees, he flings cold water on his face,
shouting into shadows, wide eyes raw

SOPHIA RIVERA

To Make Yourself Yours

I swear, there is a garden
behind the dimmed and dusty shed
that takes up too much room in your mind.
The place where you've held
all the words, faces, and traumas
you can't let go of,
even though you know
freedom will come the day you light it
with the matches your sister gave you.

Told you to use them if you ever got cold,
she didn't warn you
about where to leave shit
when all the bad started to cleave to
precious space.

You're older now,
so many years of surviving
the moon has followed you
to this place, where sacred rivers run
but the water doesn't scare you anymore.
Instead you see apparitions of your *abuelas*,
tonantzin, reflections of yourself.

When your mother tells you it isn't real
know that you will have to see for her.
Your sight will sustain you
beyond the memories of the times when
you cried and begged all night
for everything to stop
because you tricked yourself into believing
some people are just not cut out for this life.

You carry that night with you, the night that
you tried, where you wanted to and almost
did, but your *comadre* walked in
handed you a cup of water
to catch your thirst or to hold the tears.

Yet, you have made it here
to the door of the shed
to burn it down,
to clear the ash,
to walk in your garden,
and bloom.

CLAUDIA RODRIGUEZ
On Being Butch

I used to think that I wasn't pretty.
I felt that my hair was just too short, my nails jagged
in urgent need of a manicure, and my lips
and cheeks were not the right hue.

But this was before I understood and accepted
what it means for me to be butch.
Let me tell you. This butch is a *chillona* Y QUE!
who often wipes away tears
on the very same sleeve on which she's pinned her heart.

Being butch means that I'll always get, "Excuse me, this is the ladies room,"
when my bladder and temper are about to burst.
It means slipping into a fresh pair of boxer briefs—
the kind that hug my butt giving it the roundness of a small mango.
Or into a pair of *chones*—not the sexy lacy kind
but the cottony, sensible ones.
And other times I don't wear any underwear at all.
My lips rub against the seat of my jeans
and I feel the doughy softness of my inner thighs with every step I take.

It means "give me a 3 on the sides, longer on top,
square the back and *please, oh please...*
don't fuck up my sideburns."
It's been years since I've worn a dress
but my mom still wishes for the day when she'll get to see me in one...
and I wish that one day she'll start seeing me.

I'm the kind of butch that says to all you *butchas* out there
—the ones who give me and other butches the
"bitch, what-you-looking-at, I'll-drop-your- ass-in-a-minute" snarl—
please, lower your chin and relax your shoulders.
I ain't sizing you up. I'm checking you out.

Being butch means that I am definitely masculine
not to be confused with misogynist. I'm not a man
nor do I need to be to be masculine.
Women are never bitches and hoes.
Women are my *hermanas, mis amores.*
Women are another chamber
en mi corazón.

DANIELA RODRIGUEZ

A Temporary Whisper

I am contained
—Rather imprisoned—
By my own timidity
Sadly, only a few hold the key.

I think rather than speak
Because some things are better left unsaid.
And am left in the cold cement room.

Standing alone in a room full of people,
All others darken out slowly,
Leaving only me.

I am an observer
I examine
The tint of rust on old, industrial warehouses,
Notice
The daisy in a field of roses,
Marvel
At the morning dew of the lively trees and of the leaves lying on
The concrete—that will soon wither—
Stare
At the unique curves of noses.
And with the images fading quickly,
I keep to myself.

I speak volumes through art,
Which has offered me the freedom of expression
Without judgment
I give my soft words to those in my inner sanctum
I give these rare words to this poem
Only in these ways do I share the contents of my soul.

One day I will learn
To release the dormant spirit inside me,
Awaken it and let it free
It will not be meek,
Rather strong
And it will turn all heads

I will release myself of my own jail cell
But until then,
I will rattle the chains,
Attempting to noise a fraction of my soul
It echoes,
Fading quickly
Into the nothingness of oblivion.

God.
He listens to hushed prayers
Recited countless times
Until I drift asleep.
He catches the teardrops before they hit the pillow,
Giving me a temporary voice,
A temporary strength,
A temporary whisper.

NORMA RODRIGUEZ

L.A.: Story of a Transplant

TO ANDREW LAMOTTE

AT FIRST:
You are dizzying and disorienting.
The bright boldness of reds, pinks, turquoise of the beat-up store fronts
and the many colored clothes and shopping bags of homeless folks
all blend together combining to form a fast-moving dirty rainbow
glimpsed through my car window.

I have never met anyone quite like you.
There are rainbows everywhere: of traffic, of people, of buildings.
I must admit, I am a little intimidated. I am not used to you
and your L.A. fast-moving, fast-talking, rough-around-the-edges and, yet,
oh-so-casually-beautiful ways.

There are so many moving pieces, people, cars and life moving, always moving.
I try to keep up, try to look at everything all at once.
I keep asking you to slow down.

You are a rugged urban jungle that I haven't yet learned to navigate.
I still have not explored the arteries of your streets, the heart beat of your
    buildings.
I have not tasted the fruits of your street corners.

THEN NOW:
I begin to understand you, your rough-around-the-edges, fast-moving ways.
I know you are bursting at the seams with life and hope and tragedy and
    sunshine
with the dreams and the glamour and the everyday.
It all pours out of you.
Everything about you clashes, it should be a contradiction and somehow
you always manage to match your outfits effortlessly.

I am fascinated by your rhythm and pace.

You never sleep. You are intoxicating.
I don't even think about asking you to slow down anymore.
Being with you requires running to keep up with everything that you are.
I am caught up in your rainbows.

RAMIRO D. RODRIGUEZ
Dancing Through a Beating

I spin,
I squat,
Move back,
Move forward,
Take a deep breath,
And do it again.

I SPIN!
I SQUAT!
MOVE BACK!
MOVE FORWARD!
TAKE A DEEP BREATH!

Consumed by energies from the Creator,
Drenched in sweat.

The beat of the *huetl huetl*,
The rattle of the *sonaja*
My body pushed beyond its limits.
My mind focused.
And with each movement,
Every step,
I send prayers to the Creator,
My ancestors
Asking for guidance,
For wisdom
For healing,
For me,
For my family,
For my community.

I SPIN!
I SQUAT!

MOVE BACK!
MOVE FORWARD!
TAKE A DEEP BREATH!

The police handcuff me,
Spin me around,
Make me squat on the floor.
They move me back,
They move me forward,
And I take a deep breath…
With every punch that lands on my face.

Consumed by their hate,
I am drenched in my own blood.

My heart beats fast,
My bones rattle hard,
And my body has gone way beyond its limits.

Their minds are focused.

With each punch,
Every kick,
There are no prayers for guidance,
For wisdom,
For healing.

I'm only left with pain,
Shame,
Humiliation.

I SPIN!
I SQUAT!
MOVE BACK!
MOVE FORWARD!
TAKE A DEEP BREATH!

Who I was then,
Who I am now,

Who I will be,
Is all marked by the preciseness
of my ability to follow the grandfathers
into that next realm.
And on that journey,
The beat of the *Huetl Huetl* (my heart),
The rattle of the *sonaja* (my bones),
Will keep from falling off the path of the *Mexikayotl*.

I dance through the beatings of my life.
I dance through the beatings of my inner demons.
I dance through the beatings of my father's abandonment,
The choices I have made in life,
The degradation of the police.

I dance through the beatings
Of my own transitions to becoming
A strong and respected *Mexika* Warrior.

A warrior for peace.
A warrior for love.
A warrior to open doors
For our young people going forward
Into the next 7 generations,
Giving them guidance,
Wisdom,
Healing,
As they make their own transitions
On the path of the *Mexikayotl*.

So for them,
For me,
For my kids,
For my family,
For my community,
My ancestors,
Tonantzin,
Ometeotl.

I spin,
I squat,
Move back,
Move forward,
Take a deep breath,
And do it again,
And again,
And again,
And again…

TRINI RODRIGUEZ (MATRIZ)
Grown Men

Stopped at a signal
on a street outside of Home Depot
I spot a flurry of men, grown men,
the size of my *tíos*
the weight of my father
the color of everyone's brother.

They rush: one, then another, then all,
running, their sneakered feet
quickly alight on a truck,
a swarm of bees
surrounding a honeycomb of hope
desperate for dignity.

My heart breaks at this sight:
grown men reduced to mobbing a vehicle,
their ticket to money for the day
if they're lucky.
A dream turned to nightmare
pushing all up against a wall.

A once proud and able people
authorities of our own lives,
now we respond to the whim
of payers ready to spend us,
like so many prostitutes,
all in the name of a day's work.

This vision needs to end,
this parade of souls in sorrow,
this display of aching hearts,
begging for a chance to be men,
all worth their salt,
ready to put hands on any task.

So yes, our aim shifts and widens
in a knowing growing deeper:
We are 99 percent in a world off-kilter
more than flies drawn to sugar,
more than this constant running,
more than fears driving men to cars.

JEFF ROGERS
An L.A. Freeway Songbook

L.A.'s Emerald Jewelry

It's never more clear than after weeks of rain that L.A.'s a city thrown down
Into the bowls made by mountains. As I drive the freeways that thread the hills
My eyes thrill to the emerald green that rises behind buildings and presses
   the clouds.

Jam-Up on the Cat-Oh-Five

We live in L.A., city of traffic jams on the 405 and other freeways.
This morning we had three cats bunched up on the patio outside our cat door,
Competing for a lane. Elise's traffic report: "It's a jam-up on the cat-oh-five!"

Rearview Mirror Tableau, 5 Freeway South

She's passenger. He's driving.
Her face is angry and she speaks quickly.
She leans away from him. He leans toward her.

Homonculus Highway Brain Burrito

This 110 freeway with its tight lane miles I've driven so often,
Its gentle arc pass into downtown
Through high-cut banks and herky-jerky flow, must surely be wrapped in a
   myelin tortilla
In my brain—a well-traveled, intra-skull, neuronal network homunculus
   highway.

Rough Beauty

Hills driving north from L.A. on the 5 freeway display a rough beauty:
Mustard yellow, splotched with tufts of scraggly live oaks.
Hunched against drifty white clouds, skinned shoulders rust veined.

On the Braided River

Up this ramp I join the braided river, its woven flow, currents and snags.
Off right freeway bank mountains rise snow-robed.
Ahead deep pink in great daubs, across a lowering blue horizon.
Souls by the millions for miles upon miles by wordless agreements we carve
    this channel.

JEFF ROGERS

What Grows Below Ground

In tribute to Richard Duardo

That which casts out, escapes from under
The garden wall, groping blind for lands beyond.
Taproot that pushes down through seed-ground seeking source.
A time traveler of sorts, arrow tendril pointing all the way back
To that very moment when the big bang
Snapped the whole universe inside out.
That ecstasy of first creation when it explodes its banks,
From ecstatic trances of the first cave painters
Facing their rock walls rolling and swimming in firelight,
On down to us, standing here, feeling nearly deaf,
Nearly blind and nearly mute, brushes in hand
Before the empty canvas, or fingers poised above keys
Before the blank blinking screen, our arts
The coded thoughts of the universe passed through
Our twining neurons and into our hands,
Into frames on the walls before us,
Into our poems clutched in shaking fingers,
With their stutter of language, words cobbled together
From such thin and rickety letters.
How that viny S, for instance, twirls up and around,
How that scaffold E makes a ladder of three rungs from earth up to sky,
And how that Y dips its shy tail into subterranean waters below,
Then spreads its naked arms in welcome
To the rain and the star-showers above.

CONRAD ROMO

Suciopath

"*Cochino!*"
I'm maybe two
in a movie theater toilet stall with my Mom.
She's doing her business,
And closes her eyes for a minute,
while I, on hands and knees,
explore under the partition to the next stall.
My head barely pokes up
and there, perched on a toilet seat,
is a woman with her *calzones*
pulled down mid-calf.
"*Ai, cochino!*"
were the actual words
yelled at me as the woman leaned down
and slapped my face.
It was those words
that label and my face stinging
that I remember
as my first memory
in this old pervert's life.

JESSICA ROMOFF
Not Knowing What a Protest Tastes Like

I
i swear i smelt your cigarette smoke through the telephone receiver today

II
when you hung up,
i let the bathtub overflow

III
i watched the water spill and slip
into my bedroom rug. i did not touch
the faucet, even when the neighbors
complained about a leaking

IV - VI
you told me never to write
about this

VII
i wrote you a love poem. it tastes
like ash

VII a
i burnt many

VII b
taught me to forget my table manners
to eat only with my fingers

VIII
i still feel used in an empty room

IX
chapped lips, swollen knuckles,

i'm not being dramatic, i just can't
feel my knees

X
i am standing in the middle of my flood

XI
only took several minutes of heaven
to start believing in hell

XII
it's still hard to say the word "god"
with a straight face

JESSICA ROMOFF

For My Dear Naomi:
Forever 16 Years of Age

i can't imagine what it would be like
to get used to the smell of hospitals
to the sound of hospitals
rusted wheels, the squeak of latex gloves
the burning click of a life support switch turning off,
the permanent lump growing in the throat of a mother,
the last breath of her daughter
a heart monitor gone silent
the nurse made us wash our hands before we could enter your curtain

you were wedged between a young boy, with bandages plastering the left
    side of his face
and an empty bed on your right, freshly unplugged wires dangling from the sides
and there you were
the doctors still hadn't washed off everything from the crash
tubes coiled your neck, wrapped around your stomach
hunted the veins in your wrist
you were motionless
except for your chest, being inflated, then deflated by the ventilator
with this thick tube shoved between your swollen lips
you were a machine fueled by wires and electricity
yet you wore an IV like rubies
and life support like diamonds
pieces of gravel clung to your cheeks like blush
i have never seen someone more beautiful under florescent lights
i have never seen you look more like an angel than you do now

i am trying to think of your body like an obedient machine
it will keep doing what it is doing until it is told not to
i am just trying to convince myself that God pulled the plug of your lungs
and unhooked your heartbeat for a reason

God, there has to be a reason
i hate this heart monitor for being silent
i hate your eyelids for not moving
that ventilator is tapping just like your footsteps
every door is begging to be slammed
all these walls are shoving back
and this car engine is sounding too much like your pulse
and i know i can hear you
growling like a hornet's nest under your skin
i know you are there
your hand is still warm
i wish the doctors could have kissed the brain damage away
put a butterfly band aid over the 5 broken ribs
stitched up the memory loss
given it another kiss
heal

i wonder how your mother is going to spend her last night with you
nursing a vodka bottle
your home videos flooding the television
your laugh dripping onto the rug
she sings lullabies to your heart monitor
a scrapbook, the carcass, draped open on her lap like a coffin

tomorrow morning the doctors will fold you away
gently as paper cranes
softly your mother hushing you to sleep
tender as they kiss you goodbye, like a prayer to God

when she drives home from the hospital for the last time
your mother will still smell you on her sweater
in her hair
on her fingers

she will stop bathing after the funeral

Returning

You ring the doorbell
to the old house
your father grew up in,
that dark place full of clocks,
porcelain dolls, and wood
chests, carved with images
of the *carabao* in the
countryside farms. The same house
where you had your first
memories after birth.
This time you come back
with more secrets,
but with marks
that bear no likeness
to those first wounds
of childhood,
except the knowledge of things
not meant to be said.
The walls of the house
do not weep when they see you,
but offer their own stories.
The peeling wallpaper
with faded strawberry swirls;
the empty wood frames;
long windows opening
to a garden full of weeds,
old motor parts, and rusted hinges;
the long hall, and the armoire
with a mirror reflecting a woman
without a face, her long hair
the color of damp moss,
walking with a limp.
She stops to look at the ashes

of your dead grandmother,
puts her finger in the bronze pot,
and tastes the familiar.
The Virgin Mary on the altar is tired,
the prayers are too many to count,
she holds baby Jesus dressed
in a sea of black and gold lace.
His nylon curls smell like smoked fish.
There is no milk in his mouth.

POGO SAITO

Highland Park, 2 am

The bright green neon rectangle woke her from
the late night trance of being shit-caddy to an ungrateful hound:

It turned red

"BURRITOS!!"

Then, coming from 2 sides

"QUESA—   —DILLAS!!"

Flashing

"HAVE A NICE DAY!!!"

She thought about it as she walked past the battered Impala filled with
papers unfit to drive.
Unwilling file cabinet.
A lone john scurries out of a massage parlor door.
They rarely look relaxed, just ashamed and slightly less urgent.
They get lost a lot.
Wandering expectantly into dental offices and children's theaters.
Humping towards housewives and down alleys, scatting tomcats.
The neighbors see why johns pay such high rates for vacant hand-jobs
in the night.
In the morning.
Easter. Christmas. New Years Eve.
Arbor Day.
There is always vacancy for fools to pay toll.
The red and green lights shine on the window of the john's windshield:

"TACOS!"

One thing she learned living next door to johns and non-massaging whores:
They are all inconsiderate parkers. Truly. This is not a metaphor or code.
They will block your driveway in a heartbeat. Boners and commerce wait
   for no one.
The other thing she learned living next door to whores:
They drive nicer cars than artists.
They have child seats in the back of every Lexus.
The things we do for love.

The city is full of stories asleep on the sidewalk, parked on the street, stuck
    to poles
Impaled.
Stories under the overpass, passed out, passed over, past due for runaways and
runarounds found downtown, upstairs, inside, above.
Pick a preposition, a predilection, a general sort of predisposition, it's there
everywhere.
It's not just gum on the sidewalk, cigarette butts—they all came from and go
to a new tale.
A beginning. A middle. An end? Is it?
Circles and cycles and sunrise sunset, we wade in a tide of fictions
branching from a sea of secret truths:
                    "CHILAQUILES!!!"

ABEL SALAS

Talisman

If the word was inverted or the letter
took shape, the form or color that spoke
the blue or black or blood-orange tears like
the cold November rain in a pop culture
song long since forgotten, if the breath
held in a syllable of love and loss and
longing that resembles birth and death
at the same time or the pain that came
once with a phone call, your brother
crying on the other end, three states
away and your soul collapsing into
a cloud of disbelief because the baby
hummingbird you saw suffering on the
curb only days before foretold the sadness
with a whisper, a flurry and a heartbeat
racing under your fingers while you could
only lift it away and find a shaded place
for the featherless nestling to expire,
if the fear and loneliness did not return
to remind you that words and poetry
are not enough no matter how many
times a book or the printed page reminds
you that your life has been blessed, how
you have been the sum of text and type,
language spilling sometimes unchecked
across the screen or your palm in a pool
hall on the East Side where mariachis
and graying domino players make feeble
attempts to keep their demons in check,
some embracing the headlong fall into
oblivion because it helps to numb the
truth you are feeling now as you recall
being told by the most recent girlfriend

that you were everything she never knew
she wanted, as if only a lifetime ago like the
year-and-a half the honeymoons are said
to last, a story withering like an unfinished
poem or the arc a trite novella takes before
it is sadly reduced to lines like these, to
photos on Facebook and forced distance
that stings with the inevitable and the finite
realization embodied in the voluptuous
curve of a Bodoni or Garamond typeface,
the tangible document or intransigent memory
coming apart at the seams stitched together
and pressed minutes later with an iron, if
the pronunciation of desire in translation
could erase the need and the absence like
heartbreak, only then would any of this matter
because you made a pinky-swear, locked the
last digits from the beginning as if to shield it
all with a soft, symbolic talisman, protection
and power like the bone pendant she brought
you from the other side of the world, a gesture
that would bond or bubble you both, staving
off the walls like tropes of remorse that haunt
us in each lost constellation, every luminous
orb a resplendent redaction of family, friends
and loves who remain here as the objects
of dangling prepositional possibilities or an
unfinished collection of participle phrases

ALEJANDRA SANCHEZ

To My Absent Father

Today I am seeing you
your brown eyes kind, flashing with cinnamon
wrinkled at the edges
especially when you smile.
Your eyes show your lineage
China, Africa, the Philippines.

I am speaking to you of Geronimo;
you have always known him.
His big chubby fingers grasping
your fingers when he was a baby,
calling you *Lolo* (Grandfather),
hugging you at his high school graduation.
I am so proud of Gero, you are telling me
in your suit and tie
your smile a *Sampaguita* flower bursting open.
Is that what made mother love you?
(I am thinking this silently).

Later we go eat Sushi and you
arm wrestle with Gero on the table.
Gero wins; you laugh proudly.
You hold my hand
and tell me,
I am so proud of you daughter.
You say to me,
I am always here for you.

In the river, in the red   brown   white spread of wings,
holding the sky like a parachute,
nodding in approval at the *Egun* altar
with my offerings of *pansit, lumpia,* sweet sesame cakes,
coffee, and coconut milk.

Thank you,
you are telling me,
for feeding our ancestors.
Salamat po, Anaak (Thank you daughter).

Mahal kita, Itay
I love you, Daddy,
although we have never met,
not yet, maybe not ever,
I am saying this to you.

CATHIE SANDSTROM
Seven Tall Windows

Winter morning, Echo Park.
Lazing in bed I look up
from Stevens' essay
on the irrational.
Seven tall windows—
half-sky, half-hillside—
wrap the room
with wavy old glass.
Outside, steady rainfall.
I am so glad
you are not here.

Two-story white clapboard
across the hill. In its wide
north-facing window
a dark-haired woman sits
bare-shouldered, her back
to the sill. A sheet wrapped
'round her drapes in folds.
From time to time
a ghostly hand
(the artist's?)
reaches toward her,
rearranges her hair.
When she stands,
her arms press the sheet
tighter against her,
hands clasped in front.

Weather, distance and
uncertain glass distort.
How much is truth—how
much the mind's prediction,

imagination's construct.
I am compelled to watch
until rain drowns
all time-and-place
and I realize this woman
standing stripped
in the chill—I have been her.

I am so glad
you are not here.

CATHIE SANDSTROM

OK, L.A., You Win

I give.
No need to ratchet up the color
in that bright spot where the sun set.
Sunset. I saw how you silhouetted
that single palm against the sky.
Your hot-pink cirrus to lavender stratus
works every time. The surge
from melon to apricot to deepest
salmon? Unnecessary.

This long day I've stayed
at the windows, house-sitting
in Echo Park, a hillside overlooking
a wide boulevard: morning's
dazzle, pools of afternoon sun
the cat and I laze in, you
withdrawing the warmth
slowly. No star yet but
I know it's coming. Shamelessly,
you'll hang a high white moon
bright enough
to make a life by.

T SARMINA

Motel Paul Bunyan

And ever since I met Motel 6
on a California ride towards
the edge of the world
I've prayed to the gods of discount
motels, peeled paper from bars of soap
with my teeth
drank the water like it came from
blessed pipes and have eaten free ice
like it was holy bread
I've sat on the colored hills
of blue and red comforters
and watched fuzzy television
like it was a flock of sheep

When I met Motel 6
I found a church for those lost, those sacrificing
100 thread count sheets for basic empty drawers
and a bible of pamphlets of close tourist
attractions
the god of motels is called Paul Bunyan
and the origin story begins
at a place called Paul Bunyan Motel,
in a place called Porterville, CA.

And when we got there—my mother and a
six year old version of me—
Madonna was playing on the box television,
the U-Haul parked outside room 119
We arrived at that square on a map
and I pulled the curtains open
while she was sleeping
and watched an illuminated sky of
glowing vacancy signs

glowing outline of that motel god
in the sky, Paul Bunyan holding an axe
his face clean and winking

The story of pilgrims begins
with a family portrait of scenic oceans
and birds that hang on the walls of motels
This was our first family portrait
and the first home we ran to

it had a pool in the parking lot
a blue depth of 8 feet
that bred the fear of an
imaginary motel shark
bred a six-year-old fear of being
eaten right before summer

The origin story
begins with Paul Bunyan
two pilgrims
a California pair
a sleeping mother and a
six year old staying up all night to
watch a sky of blinking lights

T SARMINA

When the Sun Sits

There is a valley where the sun sits last
after sunset
after the edge of the world
has swallowed it
a valley where the sun rests
and eats

The sun will stay there one day
deaf to the calls of 5 am
and never come back

The sun will fish in the valley lake
see new colors in their scales
while we stay here
string red and blue
lights on our trees

When the sun never comes back
the light up shoes
we threw away will glow
from underneath the ground
and we'll watch them like embers
the lighting bugs of California

Our chlorine kissed hair
will be on the floor, and you'll
be able to tell what ends touched
the sun before it left

We'll remember the seasons
in museums
hair on display titled
"Summer"

The summer will be over
and they'll teach history of seasons
we'll drink coffee
with bats chirping in our windows in
the morning

We'll plug in fiber optic flowers
watch them change colors in
our front yards
spray them with flower scent

We'll draw light bulbs
rising over mountains
when the sun settles in that
last valley past the edge of the world

NICKY SA-EUN SCHILDKRAUT
Survival Mask

"we wear the mask that grins and lies . . ."

it slips on easily, slicker
than fins, soft as sea-foam,

this mask you wear the color
of flesh, an animal's shield
with a mantra: remember

to thrive in the negative,

to *burn with a hard,*
gem-like flame,

in case your heart begins
to bend, *let me in,*
let me be

no longer lonely—
this is no one else's war
you are trying to survive, but

the everyday fog of bloom and decay,

your eye an erratic camera
to each dark, cloaked body
pummeled by white-hot volts of hate,

or choked by mobs
of cops, their lists of staged suicides

that resurface along the lakes,
elegies we shout, *we do not*

forget you lived, we do
not enjoin you to forgive—

S. PEARL SHARP

Easing Into An Avenue 50 Choir

SINGING BACK TO PETER HARRIS' INSPIRATION HOUSE POETRY CHOIR

We come
easing into Avenue 50
having scrapbooked our early selves
reshaping wounds into open spaces
ready to receive droplets of
       "let it go . . .
       gonna have to let it go. . . ."

Come sliding from the freeway so
hungry for forgetting that
two words and a wail wipe us out
a ghetto whisper in red sneakers
propels us to clamor and cry
a cello plucks our sourness into sweet sweat
and we break dance with memory.
       "let it go, let it go. . ."

Years back we carried
ribs packed with deep disappointment
gut extended with cheated metaphors
ads for missing syllables painted on eyebrows
we had a terribleness then
becoming dartboards for each other's lusts
doo wops writing autobiographies from a thesaurus.

Now we come
hurts in menopause too old to bleed come
sinking to the altar of communion
receiving the wafer of word and chord
licking the last drop of drum from the glass

Between the syllables and vibrato
we clean our histories
lay down our arms for
visions we can hum
our retinas become flashlights
shining on pages simmered in simile
new hearts in old temples
singing in tongues on the Avenue
            "Got to let it go. . . ."
        singing in tongues
            "let it go . . . "
        easing into the Choir
        singing in tongues
            "let it go . . ."
        singing in tongues
        singing in tongues.

MAHTEM SHIFERRAW

Behind Walls & Glass

There are many places
where you can hide

but none are safe
for you to call home

This is a land that fed you
meat and frozen vegetables

a land that calls you
alien and immigrant

a land that defines your self-worth
by the color of your skin

a land where your language
is nothing but sounds.

How can this be home?

Isn't that a place
where you can be who you want to be

where meat comes from the goat herders
where papayas are the size of cats
where God is only God
where black & brown & white
are only colors

where you fall, and a flower blossoms
in your name

where you are not asked

if you have a nickname
if you were colonized
if your ancestors were tied & sold
to the ferrous hearts of sea merchants

if you know anyone else in the entire continent
if you were a child soldier
if you have starved

This is not it.
This is the place to hide
behind walls & glass
behind fake accents and quick smiles
behind designer clothes
& fancy cars
& lavish trips
& dancing
& nightclubs
& short shorts
& scorned boys who want to claim your body
before you know it is yours.

This is
your hiding place:

tell no one and you'll be safe.

MIKE SONKSEN (MIKE THE POET)

Blind Faith, Sour Grapes & Outside My Window

3 LOCATIONS OF POETRY

1.

Saturday started with my tour-guiding shift. I had 24 blind teenagers walking with me on Hollywood Blvd. The day's challenge involved expanding my standard descriptive capacity. They inspired me to slow down and explain the sites slower. Tactile interaction with the landscape became the mandate. They were bashful like most kids with an extra spark of inquisitiveness. They stumped me on a few questions and we did a poem south of Hollywood Blvd. They ended up schooling me.

2.

Hours later Emi, Eka & I are at the Egyptian Movie Palace to watch Totoro, Eka's favorite flick. Our seats are among the best in the house, the very back row next to the aisle. Fever is in the air, this is Eka's first time seeing it on the big screen. She knows all the lines already. We tell Eka to keep it down, she's not too loud. Still shortly into the film, a sour woman directly in front of us turns around, with a hard frown & says, "If she won't be quiet, take her OUTSIDE!" This old battered iceberg had a lot of nerve watching a children's film in a theater filled with parents & kids acting with such wickedness. Eka kept quiet after this, nonetheless I wanted to curse the woman out. Her nasty field of energy was the polar opposite of the magnanimous blind teenagers. I left it alone but it reminded me that the city is also filled with sour souls. The range is infinite in the urban electromagnetic spectrum.

3.

A few nights later, I'm up writing shortly after midnight. I hear distant cries of quarreling lovers. I do my best to ignore it, I've heard it a few times before in our neighborhood. Twenty minutes later, I hear a series of gunshots. Ka-boom! Ka-boom! Ka-boom!! Damn near a dozen shots fired, I hear it all too well. Not sure who was shot. The shooting was close to the house I know that much. I'd heard gunshots before, but this was the closest and the loudest. My heart rate immediately jumped up as a barrage of different thoughts & what-if scenarios raced through my brain. Was it that fighting couple? I thought about Emi & Eka downstairs asleep. After the sirens and ambulances came I decided to go outside and see what happened. I see a fire-truck and a dozen cop cars on Atlantic. After a few steps across the street, I think about Emi & Eka inside asleep. I decide to go back in the house. It was 1AM, I had a writing deadline and nothing but trouble could come from being outside. The next day I learned the police fired the bullets, it was an officer involved shooting; a man was shot by police after he jumped out of the car with a gun in his hand. It turned out to be the same man that was fighting with his woman earlier. The police had been called about a domestic disturbance. If he'd kept his cool he'd still be here today. I heard it all too clear right outside my window.

ROBERT STANLEY

Wounded Angels

AFTER ALLEN GINSBERG

Ever wonder?
    whose spectral legions
    colonized, legislated, then co-opted their education?

Moloch!
    pedantic Moloch!
    the smug sophist
    the landlord of daydreams
    the shameless "Pledge of Allegiance"
        and incubator of war!

Moloch!
    whose body is bloated assessments
    whose mind is soulless data and desperate flowcharts
    whose fingers craft nervous memos
    whose lungs wheeze lifeless acronyms
    whose gut belches half-baked solutions
        and whose deaf ears defer the question!

Moloch!
    in whose kindergartens they learn to read
    in whose elementary schools they love to read
    in whose middle schools they like to read
    in whose high schools they hate to read
    in whose colleges are finally allowed to read
        bold questions and honest answers.

Moloch!
    whose mission is written in smoke
    on mirrors reflecting an American dream
        untroubled by poverty.

Moloch!

        whose bells toll progress with uncertain precision
        whose religion is "numbers driven"
        whose pulpit is a PowerPoint
        whose priest is called "consultant"
        whose prime movers are billionaire dilettantes
        whose campus sets a stage for life's fiction,
                while chronic underachievers seek sanctuary for their genius!

Moloch! whose camouflage reveals
        nightmare armies!
        dishonest industries!
        hollow suburbs!
        anxious classrooms!
            and censored teachers!

Moloch!
        in whom I shout voiceless!
        in whom I am manless!
            in whom I see rows of wounded angels.

But one day!

Breakthroughs!
        down streams of common sense
        over freefalls of whimsy
        into pools of insight
            and into the streets

Ripe!
        with wild eyes
            they taste beauty
                savor truth
            and wonder…

AUSTIN STRAUS

The Good Woman of Watts

FOR WANDA COLEMAN

She is so bone good
bad people use her, take advantage.

She allows plenty of slack
on the rope you will hang yourself with.

She has trouble imagining the struggle
we regenerates have, trying to be good.

She's no innocent, far from naïve.
Her truth keeps her going.

Even when she senses or knows
what you're up to, she's tolerant to a fault.

Watches and learns, gives you multiple
chances to change for the better.

It's you who shoots yourself in the foot
or jogs off the cliff. It's you who screws up.

And it saddens her to see it. She
is so deeply decent, it hurts her

to see others fail, to feel
the causes of their failures; she strives

to illumine the roots of evil, not
even slightly tainted by its horrors.

My empress, my saintly beloved,
my woman, wife, Wanda…

AMBIKA TALWAR

Jetlag

Again I am back, floating
here in Los Angeles—not sure who I am.
Heavy is in my head
stomach, arms, feet,
and right here in my body
swathed with memory…
the dust, the smells, the fondling sounds
ma's warm-heavy hands
pa's bony shoulder my last day there
(there means Delhi, the grand old capital)
I still feel wrapped sullen by ghosts
of people I heldlovedsmelled.

Now here I sleep two–three hours
intermittently—
Pa would call me *kumbhkaran*
or *khutmull*.

This slumbering feels okay
although friends around me
think I have the virus
(they don't know jetlag).

For one week, I sleep—
waking is a lingering trauma.
I remember losing 24 hours
in delayed flights, layover in Kuala Lumpur.
Then a friend calls me from India,
we talk two–three times in 14 days;
time weaves into city sounds.

I think this is no virus
I see Delhi streets in Long Beach

I look for red letter boxes
(there I looked for blue ones)
I cook tofu, shred lettuce for salad
I unpack my bags, life's in disarray
try to readjust;
I change the clock on the side table.

I am a jetlagged yoyo
twanging on sitar strings
that sound violin-ish.

Lake Tetzcoco

This is where the journey ends.
Mexico,
is encircled by *Huaxotzinco,*
     Chalco,
     Xochimilco
     Tlacopan
     and *Cuauhtitlan.*

Here, 1521.
The salamander
crawls into
the eye socket
of a wading body.

Bodies await
as catfish
for the fishermen
to net.

The fishermen
do not weigh
their boats with fish
but a ghastly collection
of torsos,
     limbs:
owner's unknown.

The salamander
can breathe in
     water
and out of water.

It has learned

to transform
itself to aquatic or land
breather
at will.

The salamander
swishes its tail
propelling forward.
Over and around
those who
suffered the aches
of auric fever,
the righteousness
of Christianity.

Avoids the
gangrene
of those dead
who never
experienced viral infection.

The eagle, *Cuauhtli*,
has refused to land
on the cacti,
and the serpents have
gone unchecked.
The serpent and
friar hide in
and around the
basilica.
They both
have gone unchecked.

We cannot leave,
the poor and the sick.
We cannot leave
these people
to just float
in the lake.

Even if they died
like dogs.

The *Mexihcah*,
float with their hands
tied behind their backs,
obsidian hair
over puffy white eyes.

"Who is the savage,"
asks the old woman?

A cluster of infants
in a tied sack.

Three bodies,
a family,
joined together
by a single pointed lance
stuck through
their stomachs.

This is the legacy
of history,
the serpent gone
out of control,
the friar turning
his back
on Christ's
evangelical eyes.

This lake
is a steaming bowl
of human
cadavers
mulching
to say,
"Is this
the liberation of Christianity?"

Many continue
to die
because the fields
are mass graves,
and no crops
will grow.

The old ones
and the sick
wish they had
remained
as the *Axolotl*,
as the Salamander
of Lake Tetzcoco
able to go back
into the lake
and breath the
sweet water,
the salt water
of Lake Tetzcoco.

To avoid
the wrath of the sword,
shrill of the metal,
the neigh of the horse,
the necrosis of viral diseases,
and the hypocrisy
of Christianity.

LYNNE THOMPSON

Inter-mix'd

Although he chose to lie with another
and turned absent father because of it,

Daddy decided to hitch his fate to Mom.
Mother was fair in complexion (one clue

being her name—cobbled together from Low
German, middle Dutch, some old English:

hesel, hasil, hasel, hazel) but even that
hegemony didn't deter him, proud as he was

of his Igbo; proud he faced windward after
the Bight of Biafra/Bight of Bonny; pleased

to feed his family cassava & taro root. In a time
when many thought he would not have been,

he was learnéd. When he looked at her, when
she spoke her name, he might have thought

*Let the Angler fit himself with a Hazle of one piece
or two set conveniently together* (Cox, 1677)

or *the note of hasel springeth* (Hazlitt, 1864).
He might have thought of her as his hazel-wand or

hazel-hooped or a dervish of hazel-wizard healing
his scarifications, her body fully salt-fish & chickpea.

What he thought is lost to time but never can be.
He anointed himself with oil of hazel: see his

children sitting, as Virgil said, *beneath the grateful
shade which hazles, intermix'd with elms, have made?*

LYNNE THOMPSON
Émigré

Maybe it was reflex. Maybe it was memory and want—want for
the scent of soursop and sugar apples, memory of the flight of

a frigate bird, that made us drive every Sunday, down Vine Street,
past Forest Lawn Cemetery, to Griffith Park, where Daddy, nutmeg-

colored and clad head-to-toe in his all-whites, came to play cricket
and make believe he was home in Buccament Valley, St. Vincent,

West Indies, where he could be the man home would have made
of him although none of that meant one EC dollar to me because

in those days, cricket—with its ball of string & hard cork, wooden
stumps & willow-carved-blades-turned-to-bats—was just an odd British

formality, a long-ago when ladies wore pale hose and organdy hats and
I was allowed to wear my Sunday finery (as long as I didn't grass-

stain my not-for-school skirt), drink tea in Royal Crown cups and wolf
down cucumber-and-cream-cheese sandwiches those old world women

made for their men to devour during the break in the game, which
might last for a leisurely hour or more, before the teams would

take up again in a throe of fear because my Daddy was the game's best
bowler, and with his elbow cocked, and a lightning rotation of his

underarm, he threw googlies, leg-breaks, and flippers; always got his
man and took the wicket because Daddy could bring the heat—although

he never would have said *bring the heat* because his home rule kind of
schooling favored the King's English over the colloquial. But it was

exactly this heat-bringing and resplendent use of language that made
him the kind of man to be reckoned with, and I worked hard to grasp it.

MICHAEL TORRES
After I'm Gone

After I'm gone

Take me back to California

I want an open casket and the bright
ripe lemons I always talked about, in there
with me. I want everyone there. Everyone.

Tell Jonny to get a DJ and a *banda* for afterwards.
Somebody bring a bottle of Casadores; tell Jesse
to call his uncle, the Taco Man, for a favor. I hope

it'll be a long night.

People should dance *corridos*.
I would have tried to. Let the glasses clink,

not crack. If Diana shows up, ask her if everything
is alright, how she is holding up. I want to know
who misses me, who really cared. Don't you?

ANNA UREÑA

What do you mean Beverly Hills doesn't need a drone?

What do you mean Beverly Hills doesn't need a drone?
Ladies and gentleman
I am proud to present to you that on this day
July 10th 2015
that the enemy is dead
the bombs are dead too
the weapons of mass destruction are actually
missing right now but we'll get back to that later
We no longer
have a reason to fear
to fear anything on God's green earth
you can all have your 401ks back
say your prayers and go to sleep
War is over
war is over
Now it's time for peace
So now we must fight for peace
It's not gonna be easy
but if we do not stand for all that's right
in this world, then who will?
Here we come now, roll in the tanks
Line them up
Bring out the war boys
Line them up
Sound off the war drums
war drums, war drums
WAR DRUMS
WAR DRUMS
We woke up today again in a war mood
It's been centuries
when will we let it retire?

when will the refugee children come home with
the flowers they picked for their mothers? war drums
War drums as I eat
war drums as we sleep
Not working on the bomb am I?
Are we working for the bombs?
Sponsor of the bombs?
In one, out one
machine-operated-independent-witness guarded in some dungeon
    in downtown Hell
In comes the carnival of the coffins
marvels of death
as we stand on Santa Monica beach eating our hot dogs
On the front lines
all the statues are dead
We don't die in America
not unless the swine flu decides to show up again
But here come the bombs again
Here they come marching in again
Land of salute us
give us and give us
chase
that dollar

AMY UYEMATSU

The Sign Says "Closed for Business"

Word got around
to order tofu and sugar
from the Morita Grocery Company,
Grandpa Jiro's store on wheels.
On Saturdays he serviced
the entire San Gabriel Valley,
from Rosemead to San Marino,
bringing rice and milk
to the *issei* farmers who had no time
to drive into Little Tokyo.

When Jiro delivered food
in his panel truck, he'd bring
my young mother, then five or six,
to keep him company.
At each stop they'd meet a busy wife—
just enough time to gossip a little,
scribble the next week's order.
Mother remembers how popular
Grandpa was, everyone on his route
liked him—and when they got home,
a suspicious Grandma checked
his shirts for lipstick.

After Pearl Harbor, the *Moritas* were sent
on a train to Gila Relocation Camp—
built on Gila River Indian Reservation land.
Though Grandpa Jiro loved to tell stories,
he didn't talk about camp, and when
Grandpa came back in '46,
the "Closed for Business" sign
was gone—so was his store,
and all those *issei* farms
waiting for his visit.

AMY UYEMATSU

Insomnia Entry No. 24

As I hear the L.A. Times guy roar down our street at 3:30 A.M., braking
every three to four houses, I think about Sesshu reading poems on
yesterday's radio show, as he talks about a famous Zen center up north
with lovely hot springs where children aren't allowed in the water and he
wonders why such an enlightened group would turn away the glorious
sound of kids at play. Sesshu's one of those guys who doesn't go to church
but can get real quiet inside, until he brims over with some new burst and
dazzle that needs to be written down while his three little girls are running,
screaming, giggling through his house, Sesshu surrounded by the song of
women's voices, wife and daughters who don't let him get away with too much
macho and other –ismos or –isms. And it's all good, that's the thing.
Sesshu's yelling "motherfucker" and "hey, look at this" in one breath, the
injustice and the gorgeous exploding in every direction he turns. And it's
all good, his poems so convincing, when you can laugh through all the shit,
learn how to cook your own brand of menudo, keep the game ball rolling
as long as you can.

Homie

Smokes a Camel and spits on the hot asphalt. He
raps his story out the side of his mouth. Wife-beater
under a hoodie, *gordo* brother's pants, legs cut to fit.
Holy Mother of universal exultation holds cathedral's
door, but there's no road in the shadow of her wings.
Mama's cancer cure, relief from Dad's belt buckle,
unanswered prayers. He must blaze his own trail across
Zanja Madre. Sun roasts the air above L.A. River bridges.
Smog hangs with charcoal smoke from the San Gabriel's
wildfires, acrylic sunset paints the Heights in oranges
and lemons, like crime scene tape. Colt 45 night-cap on
moist night grasses of Plaza De La Raza in twilight, he curls
down on the damp sod. Dream song lyrics punctuated
by *chingada* between syllables. Hollenbeck Division *putos*
sweep the park in rubber gloves, Waistband 9 his only peace.

ROLLAND VASIN (VACHINE)
How?

If a boy of Japanese ancestry from Gardena was sent with his parents to concentration camp in Wyoming for the duration of World War II, and upon arrival his baseball bat was confiscated so he never played baseball again,

if a brother and sister from Boyle Heights were jeered as Mexicans, and told to go back to where they came from, but they and all their Indigenous ancestors, for as far back as anyone could count, came from Boyle Heights,

if a black girl from Mississippi watched her father dragged from his house in the middle of the night, by men in bed sheets, hanged on a poplar tree and his mutilated body set on fire with gasoline, so every time she fills the tank of her car in South-Central, and smells gas, she sees her Dad on the tree,

how do these citizens abandon the desire to punish their tormentors long enough to earn a Nobel Peace Prize, be confirmed as a Justice of the Supreme Court, finish school?

How do we move from them to we? How do we embrace as family?
How do we all say God Bless America?

How?

hybrideities

Kukulcán
Quetzalcoatl
hybrid names for a hybrid god

This millennium
brings in its basket of goodies
more hybrid names
for bridges
people of hope:

GuateMayAngelino
GuanaMex
Guanachapín
GuanaChapílena
GuanaChapiMex
ChapiCano
GuaCatraChapicana
GuaNiCatraChapicano
TicoGuanaCatraChapicanAngelina

and the list continues . . .
as does our struggle
and our hope

Quetzalcoatl
Kukulcán
nombres híbridos
deidad híbrida

este milenio
trae en su costal
más nombres híbridos
para gente especial

puentes de esperanza
entre nuestras comunidades

GuateMayAngelino
GuanaMex
Guanachapín
GuanaChapílena
GuanaChapiMex
ChapiCano
GuanaCatraChapicana
GuaNiCatraChapicano
TicoGuanaCatraChapicanAngelina

y la lista continua…
al igual que la lucha
y la esperanza

VICKIE VERTIZ

1. Postcard from My Father

Mija! You should have been there!
The boxer knocked him out
Like that, flat on the floor asleep
Bien chingon, se cree el cabron

Dance with me, *chata*!
"*Me dicen que estoy loco,*
Pero estoy loco por ti"

I'll jig without you then
Whistle whistle! What a riot
Change the channel
More fights are coming on

Wish you were here, *mija*
Come on, don't get all feelings on me
I may be drunk
But at least I'm home

I could be scrambled
eggs on the freeway
or tipsy into the Bufadora cave
hitting every rock with my face
making *ceviche*
out of me

VICKIE VERTIZ

2. Postcard to My Father

Under a Eucalyptus tree
Mourning doves succor
Chicks in a nest and one falls out hungry
They leave it there, maybe for later

Dust tracks across the rocks
I wish you were here

You wade in ponds of car grease
Elbows bloodied
From scraping against cinder blocks
From scooting on a skateboard away from us

I'm on vacation and I don't drink
You eat the *menudo*
for both our hangovers

Hold your head up
it's about to roll off

I wish you were here
napping on a blue-green blanket
Mom popping the pimples on your back

I wish you were
Less thirsty

You interrupt
Sing sticky drunk
"*Dicen que estoy loco*
Pero estoy loco por ti"
But your song is not about *Amá*
It's for the one in Tijuana
And her flat-nose daughter

But I'm not a girl anymore
Instead of staying to watch you
Open another can
I leave in my car
Just like you used to

JENNIFER LISA VEST

When I was Born

When I was born
King was planning his march on Selma
Kennedy was inaugurating
The NASA space program
And my parents were catching
Hell from realtors who didn't want to
Sell a house to an interracial
Couple

My father says he was doing
His part to change things
By bringing a series of
Little mixed babies
Into the world

But my mother was
Afraid of the lives
We would be forced
To live

Because of desegregation
Affirmative action
My light skin
My mother's long hair
And King's people marching
I got educated I got a chance
I am a success story

People who don't know me
Find me beautiful
People who do know me
Don't understand

When I was born King said
Things still aren't right in Selma
And look 35 years later
They still aren't right

But
I shouldn't complain
Because my mother was wrong
Or was she right?
About the life I would
Be forced to live

ESTELA VICTORIA-CORDERO

Concrete Love

I should love you city knowing you are nature
Molded by hands, all of these sands, we are wanting more
Wanting a place to stay, a place to play
People need you, concrete please rise

Rise by the dark hands of the *Obrero*
Designed by the minds of the *Guero*
You become a sparkling pool of lights
At night, when the sun hides ashamed

Why should we love you, concrete, love?
Because from the earth you came
Natural rock we hit you hard, then we cracked and knocked
Till you fell down in a heap, sliding, sliding

We then took you in our powers
And hit you, smashed you, added stuff to you
You were nothing to us, but a bunch of powder
And we wanted to do more, so we pushed you harder

Into a sludge so ugly, but you are natural still you know
You wait patiently in those trucks, to be towed
You know your fate is to be, what we want to see
Our homes, our buildings, we rest our heads

Why do you look so ugly then, up close,
And so beautiful from far away? You are nature still aren't you?
Cities are beasts, our Frankensteins, we have to live with you,
In you, for you, we therefore love you, Concrete Love

ANTONIETA VILLAMIL
Evening Snapshot

On Sunset Boulevard   avoiding
the fanfare of actors' trivial lives   thwarted
moon drifting from stupid head of sun
billboard   to *chihuahua* taco placard
in the Godzilla mouth of dusk   like adolescents
over portabella mushroom sandwiches
and lemon grass tea   gorging on reckless
gestures   engaged ears over gossip
Not paying attention to the clock in despair
of late schedules   Astonished at how the signboard
especially the cul-de-sac of it   resembles
a contemporary sculpture to the red bell peppery
architecture of twilight   and the end of day
fastened to the codes of talking silken   the blast
of walking gay   festering sun of Hollywood behind
tourists   babbling childlike   over the last potato fry

ANTONIETA VILLAMIL
America Malinche's Trade

In the past the Princess Malintzín, or Malinche, was sold as slave and delivered as proof of submission to the Conqueror Hernán Cortés. At present and heading to the United States, a Latin-American woman puts on the shoes of the Malinche, to talk about how mother earth is usurped and sold to the highest bidder.

I trade the ice of your new moon for a spark of my tropic in your groin. I swap the wink of my comrade eye for the neat impatience with which you entice me. I exchange the sizzling salsa of my hips, the jazz of my hot word in your ear, a thick fragrant coffee at dawn, for nothing, not even thanks.

I trade the peace of a breakfast with tortilla or corncakes and milk chocolate for the North of your loneliness that drips fortified cereal for hunger. I swap the art wealth of my cuisine for your cancerous soda and your mad cow burger with emaciated white bread. I give you my lover heart, the unquestioned pleasure of a thousand and one nights, a Kamasutra in Spanglish and the adoration of how many women you want, for an iota of peace.

I exchange the horror of the disappeared and those who dig in the mines their own grave, for the unconditional diamond of a profound free dream. I have put my black gold, my 24-karat gold, my nuclear energy, my emeralds, my cotton, my coca gold and the poppy's dream.

I have put my land and my working people at your disposal. Now I put my eye for your eye, my tooth for your tooth. I lay down my life. I put my diversity in exchange for your indifference. All you have wanted I have been giving you in exchange for a promise: an equitable destiny, legal and free from pollution. *Una situación de gano y ganas.* You win if I win. You know it well, my adorable conqueror, that nobody loses with *fair trade.* Moreover, with all your power in this game of death at the end, no one takes a single toy
    to the grave.

CELIA VIRAMONTES

A Book All My Own

"Ten is the maximum," the librarian says
sliding the shiny square card and a pen across the counter,
pointing to the blank space, where I press pen against plastic to sign my name.
I sprint to the children's area where books are shelved like dominoes
ready to drop in my hands.
Mamá flips through magazines in the "*Libros en Español*" section,
ESL practice manuals that promise *inglés rápido*,
an illustrated book on *la historia de México*, for Papá.
A book on butterflies falls on my lap, monarchs leap off the page,
circling me and Mamá, ready to follow us home.
One by one, they spill into my hands:
exotic parrots in distant lands, books by E.B. White,
blooming orchids, stories from far and wide.
At the check-out desk, the librarian takes my card,
swipes my new-found discoveries on a scanner,
stamps the due date on a white paper strip,
old "return by" dates scratched out in pen.
"Enjoy!" he says, revealing his pearly teeth,
lined up like dominoes across his mouth.
I tuck my library card in my back pocket,
zigzag out the library with Mamá,
past East L.A *washerías*, *panaderías* and corner liquor stores
heaving ten books in my arms.
I will do it all again, next Saturday,
and the Saturday after that
dreaming of the day I will have a book all my own.

CELIA VIRAMONTES

Hunger

"*Qué se te antoja?*" Mama asks one spring day, a spatula in hand.
But it is impossible to answer,
I fancy anything that is made with Mamá's hands.
So she shuffles through cupboards,
drawers, a refrigerator until she's gathered
pumpkin and *ajonjolí* sesame seeds, chile *negro, mulato,* and *guajillo*
hojas de laurel, chocolate, *piloncillo,*
almonds, *pollo,* a roll of *bolillo.*
I rush into the kitchen to help my 'Amá but
she nudges me back to the nook in our couch
to study my fourth grade spelling bee words.
Hours later, I've practiced words like A-L-C-H-E-M-Y and A-L-L-U-R-E
and sniff my way back to 'Amá's side, lured by the
red thick sauce bubbling up to the top of the *olla.*
"*Un poquito espeso y picoso,*
dulce y sabroso," Mamá chants an *adivinanza.*
She stirs and stirs, lifts the spatula dripping with the
sizzling burgundy blend to my lips
as I contemplate her riddle.
A bit thick and spicy,
sweet and savory?
"*Mole!*" I guess through a burned tongue.
And just like that,
Mamá feeds
my hunger
and my imagination.

MELORA WALTERS

Nature Poem, #5

The night is dark
crickets saw out their call
to ask the night to back off
and leave it alone.
There is one frog
close to the house.

The liars sit in their beds
holding electronics close to their chests

like missals from the middle ages

counting how many prayers will get them
closer to heaven.

—

Liars.

with so many games
changing rules.

Liars.
—

An idiot
a rabid animal
froth at the mouth
runs through the woods
a flower caught
in a torn ear
unbrushed hair
glassy
red eyed

mistaking a tree
for a giant
or a saint.

The crickets continue to saw.

I sit and curse.
I hit the ground.
I stamp the ground.
I rail against the black sky.

The crickets continue to saw.

I promised.
I lived up to my promises.
I begged forgiveness.
I punished myself.

The crickets continue to saw.

I stayed true to the course.
I did everything you asked.
I researched different gods.
I gave them all food.

The frog croaks.

And you left me.

The crickets saw.

The wind is a buffalo robe.

The crickets sing.

A house in the desert
silk flags tied to poles
an exquisite sculpture
carved in sand

bejeweled
to an unknown goddess.

The crickets sing.

The frog moans.

It is no different from when I was 10
riding my bicycle against the shamal
marks on my skin.
I rode home to those people
no different than these.

The crickets and frogs are silent.

It will be light soon.

HILDA WEISS
Before the Long Weekend

Here comes the spot on the road where wheels grind.
But no fear. It's not the engine failing
on a curve halfway to Malibu. It's the road,
sanded and scraped of hardened oil,
craving a new surface.

Like summer when you towel down and skin
peels in little rolls that make you
hum and shiver. Like jazz on the radio.

A girl in pink flip flops and lemonade dress.
Crows carrying long grass.
What's That? A New Something. Oh Baby,
How Are You? Lavender sky, new
crescent moon. Sand me.

Dive into my bones.

HILDA WEISS

The Poem

Sometimes it has white hubcaps
and turquoise flames down its panting
white sides. The roof
cracks open like butterfly wings.

Its metal has a way of lasting.
I've seen it in a black limousine,
all polished hips and shoulders and
a woman in high heels—
her tight, muscled calves.

I've been taken on its slow drive
uphill, in silence. I waited,
overlooking the city while it undressed.

Sometimes in tall grass—
a hummingbird on the radio antennae—
I've seen its hulk rise
towering with satisfaction,
like a woman turned ninety.
See—her face steadies
so quickly. She forgets everyone.

SAMMY WINSTON
Sambas

He stood with his back to the cross, lost in thought. A sack of sour worms in one hand. A burning blunt in the other. His bowed head bobbed metronomic nods as he muttered muddled hymns from memory. A fitting tribute to the abandoned church we had squirreled into. Embedded in the pews, I was stewed on the electric pink brew of dirty Sprite on chipped ice, gripped tight in a Big Gulp cup. Droopy loopy and deep within in my druid hoodie, I watched him in his odd little trance. His big eyes danced behind their half-mast lids as his lips twisted around whispered phrases of praise of a deity which we neither much believed in.

Lost boys roaming the humdrum summer, another gloaming approaching hot on our asses. The dusk sun was running from us delinquents in that shadow-dappled chapel in the hills, and it was made of fire, and yet it still seemed like something we could leap onto. A step away, as simple as minding the gap on a subway platform. Wander around. Ride it down to yakuza towns.

A cat getting fucked somewhere outside sounded like silver screen infanticide, but the spell broke, and he awoke, hoisting double thumbs up without dropping his stuff. Smooth as a June breeze, he moved through the half-light of the room on mack-slack legs whose lackadaisical shoes toed empties and butts from his way. Shadows shifted as planets drifted, and the sun's fall was fast, and burglar beams of moonlight quickly cast a mother of pearl swirl onto our scene.

When he finally faced the cross on the wall, his aura lost all sense of play; the hazy revelry of reverie had wholly drained from his teenage face. His lazy gaze honed up dart sharp; keen in the eyes and mean at their brows. He aimed two accusatory fingers at the skinny little man on the wood, who had promised free-will but not fair-play, and he pushed his first original words of the evening through touching teeth, growling, "I want my friends back from their graves."

TERRY WOLVERTON

Work

Woman on her knees before the big clock.
Morning is no peach pie, no lemon sun.
Light the new day with violet lanterns,
she begs another sky, its coral roof.

Same story, the room always waiting; hot,
its breezes sour, chemical. Day begins
before the candle melts. Even the dog
on the grounds remembers his zone of rope.

The schedule is turning in her brain,
minutes hanging from dry, tired trees, doubting
theories of twilight. Is she a person
or an explosion in the factory?

The wrong moon colors this night; all the birds
in the green world cannot release her earth song.
Time's sad machine still starts and stops. Dinner
in the shade of the flame lit universe.

NANCY LYNÉE WOO

The Disappearing Act

There for the first 38 years
       all witch bone
       tea leaves
       thin wrists
         the voices

Hard, mean face
       punishingly beautiful
       snap stick on knuckle
       crack crack crack
         when they were bad

Sirens in second story
South Central flat
two bedroom two boys
there must have been some
       love
in those chopsticks

There for the first 38 years
       and then, gone

Not vanished
      (the last time   my father   saw her
           face   was in   1988.
           It was   ambulance red
         wailing   &   damning him
                             to hell
         this time   his wife
                      his life)

but slammed
       into hard, white dust.

Gone
except for the

crack
        crack
                crack

of wrong

NANCY LYNÉE WOO
Reflection

cold snap of bone, the pig's leg breaks
rice steams over pork belly, hissing

I didn't grow up near a river
but I know the silence of leaves

coal stoves heat scraps under straw roofs
a cold migration to suicide factories

I see a bride in wooden sandals
a poet missing her in the forest

a great wall built by slave hands
and a child beaten by the fire

for crying too loud, shush
there is always a war outside

that someone is protesting
a tank in a village, the emperor's robes

and loud-mouthed innocence
almond eyes unblinking in the glass

GAIL WRONSKY
Dolphins Are People, Too

Before Marlena strung crystals and mirrors in our trees
so that when the wind blew crazy light flashed off in all

directions, before Peter made a song bow out of locust
wood and played it against his head which worked like a

sounding box when he hit the bow's one string with his
pocket knife, before the mean old macaroon-maker was

kicked out of Hell, before no one answered the question,
before Topanga meant Mountains to the Ocean, before

dark clouds rose in the south, before Galileo looked
through the peephole, before somebody took my sister's

fa-sol-la and made it a nightmare, before any man loved
a woman, before the *comandante* went to jail, before

Dan put the salt and pepper in his poetry which before
that had had a lot to say about trains coming or trains

going or people getting on and off of trains, before tweed
jacket boredom, October, gunfire, Nigeria, or 1966,

before the wildest hour shook its violet hair out all over
the evening mountains, before the car horn and the barking

dog and the homeless guy playing flute in the lot next to
Moon's Market, before fat cows and robbed graves, before

Mozart, before glitter showered down on the disco floor
like the promise of enduring love, before you wanted

anything, before the hunter Actaeon saw the goddess Diana
bathing naked in the lake for which transgression she made him

a stag, before the stag was chased down and dismembered
by dogs he had until that minute owned, before faster was

not necessarily better, before Cleopatra met Julius Caesar,
Mark Antony, *or* death, before the baby swallowed the tiny

corner of window pane, before Santa Ana winds sliced in
through the kitchen window, before Crazy Horse had his

crazy horse dream, before coffee filters, Kafka, slavery,
Sweet Georgia Brown, and the *Mahabarata*, they all said the

heck with it and walked into the Pacific, their arms
disappearing, their hands slanting off into fins.

GAIL WRONSKY

And in green meadows raise a purple temple

The sound you hear it's a hammer chiseling time out of fragrance and our
pain it's a *pas de deux* of childhood dreams and generations' claims it's the

dance of a sand-grain in the stem-crook of a shoreline flame or it's you and
me pulling ourselves along an infinite chain of incongruities toward

unthinkable death (oh tissued scrim of history a skeleton man with a look of
pity asked me up to his apartment the best in New York City) that was long

before we fell into the *ayahuasca* lord and now that we've lost our talent
for impersonating lizards now that we've harvested for ourselves the long

green hair of a river now that we've pawned our ethnic jewelry from Cuzco
and Costco where's the poem that once held it all for us all pleasure and

all sense and what is this over-intended sandwich of canned meat "boneless,
economical" oh monuments oh polychromatic Kali lying moldering and
silent at our feet

TINA YANG

Why My Mother, the Bald Headed Nun, Rejected Me

When my mother was small that bamboo stick the math teacher bore
down on her lat top head with a sharp crack like gum chew knocked the
numbers from her head as well as her hairpiece was what my grandmother
her mother told me growing up. It was his fault Grandmother said as if all
the yam leaves my mother forced herself to devour wouldn't have bleached
her olive toned skin and her illegitimacy any other way but at least they
grew her hair back. My mother the belle of the ball. Before she gave up her
rough countryside tongue for the smooth egg salad of Americanese she
would eat cherry pie. She called out at raucous bingo games laughed loudest
with prim Republicans grew her thick moonlit tresses down to her waist then
rejected a Cal Tech graduate with body odor like mildew. He went on to
be the Bill Gates of China and married a woman who stuffed her nose with
tissues and called him pretty. My father had his pick of ladies in tight dresses
and brought my mother a box of chocolates before knocking her up all one
hundred forty five pounds four foot nine of her. She saw the light of Buddha
one day shining like crude yellow gold from a dead fish's eye only to realize
that there was life developing in her. Working graveyard shift as a computer
technician in the late seventies put the drag queen makeup on her face
while her belly swelled and her husband cheated on her with all of
Chinatown. Miss Taiwan American Twelfth Runner Up lived twenty-one
paces from where dogs howled from their cages and ate tomatoes carved in
the shape of rabbits. By then she was down to eighty five pounds and fell
asleep on her mother's waterbed chanting Sutras waking up only to tease her
hair into coarse tight poodle curls. Not yet into the Holy Land my mother
fulfilled her Confucian duty when I came out covered in amniotic fluid
grimacing like a gargoyle.

TINA YANG

Beautiful

Hey, and the squatty imitation Rhett Butler
on the corner winks big.
I wheel around, glare defiantly;
I give him the finger.
Years later the guy with a jagged bowl
cut, tan bomber jacket,
emerges from the darkness one inky night.
You have the kind of face I want
to rub all over and lick, he says;
Wide hips. Marry me.
I'm tall, dark, and some say,
Oh, you will just pass for cute.
Revolted, I run;
hide down in a library
basement till closing time.
Maybe it was seeing
the sharp features soften,
like spring awakening.
You, leaning on your elbows,
whisper:
Beautiful,
you're so beautiful.
My God, how beautiful you are.
Your long fingers delicately trace
my forehead to my chin.
Under your gaze of wonder,
I withdraw into myself, the rotund girl;
like a woman retreating
down a chilly cul-de-sac
but looking back,
the street lamplights
turning her eyes amber.

MARIANO ZARO

My Mother Wakes Up Late

My mother wakes up late these days.
I help her to get up. I put on her glasses.

We walk to the bathroom. Twenty five steps, slowly.
I hold both her hands as if we were dancing.
She brushes her feet against the floor.
I walk backwards.

It is kind of cloudy today. She says that every morning
since her sight started to fail.

She sits on the toilet, rubs her eyes,
runs her fingers through her hair trying to remove
the remains of last night's medication.

I am about to prepare the bath. *What is that?* she says.
There is a dead moth in the bathtub.

How is she able to see it?
She cannot read anymore,
she cannot sew—she loved sewing,
cannot watch TV—it bothers her eyes.
She still has good peripheral vision.
The doctor has told me.

The moth has left a trail behind—golden, glittery.
Calligraphy written by a drunken hand.
A trail of dance and death.

It's just a moth, mother. They come in at night. I tell her.
I clean the bathtub with toilet paper. I let the water run.

I start to remove my mother's night gown.
Five buttons on her chest.
This must be the end of summer, she says.

Acknowledgments

"Iftar Streets" and "Haze" by Tanzila Ahmed were part of an annual project called "Poetry a Day for Ramadan"—an online writing group that writes poems daily during the holy Muslim month of Ramadan.

"In Los Angeles" by Li Yun Alvarado was previously published in the chapbook *Nuyorico, CA*.

"Three Minutes with Mingus" by William Archila was published in *The American Poetry Review*.

"The Boys of Summer" by Xochitl-Julisa Bermejo was published at *Poet's Responding to SB 1070* and *La Bloga*.

"Hollywood Hills Noir" and "Blue Smoke and Steel" by Laurel Ann Bogen are from *Psychosis in the Produce Department: New and Selected Poems, 1975-2015* (Red Hen Press, 2016).

"Being Human" by Jessica M. Wilson Cardenas was published in her poetry book *Serious Longing* by Swan World Press.

"Sonnet for Austin" by Wanda Coleman is from *The Love Project: A Marriage Made in Poetry* by Wanda Coleman and Austin Straus (Red Hen Press, 2014).

"Driving Late at Night in Hollywood with a Foreign Visitor" by Carol V. Davis is from *Between Storms* (Truman State University Press, 2012).

"An Addiction" by David M. Diaz was previously published in "American Mustard: Volume 1" (Lulu).

"Fontanel" and "Workout" are from Kim Dower's third collection, *Last Train to the Missing Planet* (Red Hen Press, 2016).

"Queer" by Christian Elder was published previously in *Blue Satellite Magazine*.
"My Name on Top of Yours, #14" by Yvonne M. Estrada was published in *My Name on Top of Yours*, poetry chapbook (Silverton Books, 2013); "The Coyote in the Living Room" was published in *Yay! LA* (April, 2015).

"When Called in for Questioning" by Rich Ferguson was previously published in *Cultural Weekly*.

"The Night Nurse" by Jamie Asaye FitzGerald was previously published in *Mom Egg Review*.

"Like My Mother" by Angela Rose Flores has been published in the "Madre, Mother" issue of *Mujeres de Maiz Flor y Canto Zine*, 2015.

"Closing Prayer" by Michael C. Ford recorded as a soundtrack on a LaserDisc video titled "LA Journal" for the Voyager label in New York, 1997. Also published as a print document in the New Mexico periodical *Mas Tequila Review*, 2010.

"Meet Me at the Lighthouse" by Dana Gioia first appeared in *Virginia Quarterly Review* in 2015.

"Buñuelos" by liz gonzález was published in *Art/Life*; Lummis Day Souvenir Program, June 2008; and Silver Birch Press's *My Sweet Word Series*.

"In The Valley" by William A. Gonzalez was previously published in Gonzalez's poetry collection *Blue Bubblegum: Sticky Literature* (Xlibris, 2015).

"Water and Power" and the "Politics of Memory" by Kevin Hearle are reprinted from *Each Thing We Know Is Changed Because We Know It, and Other Poems* with the permission of the author and the Ahsahta Press of Boise State University. "Water and Power" was originally printed in *Crazy River #3*.

"How to Sell Your First Screenplay and Become Rich" by William Ryan Hilary first appeared in *A Fine Flu* (Spring 2015); "Poems from the Bargain Bin" first appeared in *Junk 4* (Summer 2011).

"This Small Thing" by Alexandra Hohmann appeared in *Yay! LA* magazine (online).

"all the characters" by Boris Ingles posted online under *Cadence Collective*.

"Poster Boy" by Gerda Govine Ituarte was published in online magazine *Dryland Los Angeles Arts and Letters*.
"Rain" by traci kato-kiriyama previously published in "Signaling" by *The Undeniables* (2010).

"-ING" by Douglas Kearney was published in *Public Pool* (Red Hen, 2015).

"Los Angeles" by Janice Lee previously published in *Entropy* (July, 2014).

"Temple" by Kimberly Lieu will be included in her forthcoming, self-published book *Funeral Songs*.

"February 14" by Phoebe MacAdams was published in *Strange Grace* (Cahuenga Press, 2007).

"Mom's War Stories (version 4)" by Robert Mäder-Kammer was previously published in *A History of A Journeyman Poet* (Author House, 2015).

"Real Days Off" by Bill Mohr first published in *Blue Collar Review: Journal of Progressive Working Class Literature* (Spring, 2008; Volume 11, Issue 3); "Complexities" first appeared in *CQ: California State Poetry Quarterly*.

"Promenade at Dawn" and "Santa Monica Farmers' Market" by Majid Najicy were previously published in *Iranian.com* and *Iroon.com*.

"East Hollywood 3" by Harry E. Northup has been posted on *timestimes3.blogspot.com* and published in *East Hollywood: Memorial to Reason*; "Young Latina writes in her journal" has been posted on *timestimes3.blogspot.com*.

"Caves of Los Angeles" by Martin Ott previously published in *Weber—The Contemporary West* and *Underdays* (University of Notre Dame Press); "California is Sinking" published in *The Normal School*.

"From the Permanent Collection: Self Portrait With Roadside Grave Marker" by Candace Pearson appeared in *West Trestle Review*.

"The Pursuit of Happiness" by Holly Prado appeared on the literature/arts blog *timestimes3.blogspot.com*.

"Gasoline Dreams" by Arturo Quiros was featured online on *Soundcloud* and *Colorlines*.

"Fingerprints on Tortillas" by Luivette Resto previously published in *She Did it Anyway* (In the *Words of Women International Anthology*, 2015).

"Night Rituals" by Thelma T. Reyna originally published in *Spectrum* (Palabra Productions: L.A.).

Earlier versions of "LA Freeway Songbook" by Jeff Rogers appeared in the "Three Line Lunch" series at fierceandnerdy.com and the "Words of Fire" series at capitalandmain.com. An earlier version of "What Grows Below Ground" was a winner of the Lummis Day Festival 2015's "Back to the Roots" contest honoring Los Angeles artist and printmaker Richard Duardo, published by the City of Los Angeles Department of Cultural Affairs with the Arroyo Arts Collective as a postcard giveaway to festival attendees, backed with a Duardo print. The festival winners are also being published in *NELA Art News*.

"Returning" by Melissa Roxas was first published in *Rhino Poetry*.

"Motel Paul Bunyan" by T Sarmina featured in performance piece, "but what you want is far away" presented by the Oakland Museum of California and SFMoMa, also published by Nomadic Ground Press. "When the Sun Sets" featured at the Oakland Museum of California, a project of Poet's House.

"Behind Walls & Glass" by Mahtem Shiferraw is scheduled to be published in 2016 in a chapbook by the same title from Finishing Line Press.

"The Good Woman of Watts" by Austin Straus is from *The Love Project: A Marriage Made in Poetry* by Wanda Coleman and Austin Straus (Red Hen Press, 2014).

"Émigré" by Lynne Thompson was first published in the *African American Review*; "Inter-mix'd" was first published in *Spillway*.

The excerpt in the introduction from "Fire in the Village" by John Trudell is from *Lines from a Mined Mind: The Words of John Trudell* (Fulcrum Publishing, 2008).

"The Sign Says 'Closed for Business'" by Amy Uyematsu published in *The Yellow Door* (Red Hen Press, 2015); "Insomnia Entry No. 24" published in *The Asian American Literary Review*.

"hybrideities" by GusTavo Adolfo Guerra Vásquez was published in *Desde el EpiCentro: An Anthology of U.S. Central American Poetry and Art*, edited by Maya Chinchilla and Karina Oliva-Alvarado (Los Angeles: Epicentro, 2007).

"Postcard from My Father" by Vickie Vertiz was published as "Postcard from My Pops" in *Huizache*.

"Work" by Terry Wolverton was previously published in "Curator's Essay" by Ariadni A. Liokatis, *Drawn to Language*, exhibition catalogue, USC Fisher Museum of Art. Los Angeles, CA, 2013.

"Dolphins are People, Too" by Gail Wronsky was originally published in *Askew Journal;* "And in green meadows raise a marble temple" was originally published in *Yew Journal of Literature and Art.*

"Why My Mother, the Bald Headed Nun, Rejected Me" by Tina Yang was previously published in the anthology *It's Animal But Merciful* (MEDIA Publishing House, 2010).

"My Mother Wakes Up Late" by Mariano Zaro has appeared in the following publications: *Askew* (Ventura, CA) and *Colorado Blvd. Magazine* (online).

Contributors

INTRODUCTION

Luis J. Rodriguez is founding editor of Tía Chucha Press, which has been publishing culturally rich, socially engaged poetry books for 27 years, and co-founder of Tía Chucha's Centro Cultural & Bookstore. He is currently Poet Laureate of Los Angeles.

POETS

Ricardo Lira Acuña earned his BA from Stanford University in English and French Literatures and his MFA from Columbia University in Screenwriting. Ricardo has published two books of poetry and photography: *under the influence* and *Greetings from Heaven & Hell*. His poetry has been published in *The Los Angeles Times*, *Altadena Poetry Review: Anthology 2015*, *Lowriting: Shots, Rides & Stories from the Chicano Soul*, *Yellow Medicine Review*, *PALABRA: A Magazine of Chicano & Latino Literary Art Issue 6*, *Los Angeles Latino Heritage Month Calendar*, among other publications. rickyluv.com

Thomas Adams has taught secondary English for LAUSD for twenty-five years to students grades 7-12. He is developing an after school course at Sylmar High School that he hopes to get accredited, and is introducing the spoken word poetry of the *Get Lit: Words Ignite* program. He lives in Simi Valley with his wife and three children (who are no longer children).

Tanzila "Taz" Ahmed is an activist, storyteller, and politico based in Los Angeles. She can be heard monthly on the #GoodMuslimBadMuslim Podcast. She wrote a "Radical Love" column at loveinshallah.com for the past two years, was a long-time writer for *Sepia Mutiny*, and is published in the anthology *Love, Inshallah: The Secret Love Lives of American Muslim Women*.

Nelson Alburquenque is the rhythm guitarist for the alternative rock band *Tikal Sun*. He is 26 years old and resides in North Hollywood, California.

Rosie Angelica Alonso was born in East L.A and recently earned her Master's degree in poetry from California State University, San Bernardino. Her poetry recounts stories of the working class people in the barrio, the myths of *La Virgen Roachalupe*, and the overlooked Chicano punk culture in East Los Angeles.

Karina Oliva Alvarado currently teaches in the Chicana/o Studies department at UCLA. Born in El Salvador, raised in Little Central America, she has written poetry throughout most of her life. She is also an artist.

Li Yun Alvarado is a Nuyorican poet, scholar, and educator living in Long Beach, CA, where she teaches English at Long Beach City College. She is the author of the chapbook *Nuyorico, CA* and her work has been published in journals and anthologies including: *Wise Latinas: Writers on Higher Education*; *Kweli*; *The Acentos Review*; and PALABRA: *A Magazine of Chicano and Latino Literary Art*. She is an Acentos Fellow and has participated in the VONA/Voices writing workshop and Astra Writing in Greece.

Dr. Melissa F Alvarado was born in Nebraska. She published in Haight Asbury's literary publication, *SIC 3*, and hosts the Nebraska Lit Girl Hour, where she interviewed Laurel Ann Bogen, Molly Peacock, and Nathalie Handel. She is creator of the Nebraska Lit Girl reading series at Beyond Baroque.

Rafael F J Alvarado was born 1965, right below Sunset and Vine in Hollywood. His grand-uncle was a great poet of Guatemala; his grandmother was also a poet. Rafael is blessed by the birth of his son, Maximo.

Unapologetic feminist, dulcet-toned poet, activist, film-maker, editor of *Zestyverse* (LossLit), **E. Amato** is a published poet, award-winning screenwriter, and established performer. She has three poetry collections released by Zesty Pubs: *Swimming Through Amber*, *5*, and *Will Travel*, and is a content writer for *The Body is Not an Apology*.

William Archila is the author of *The Art of Exile* (Bilingual Review Press, 2009) which won an International Latino Book Award in 2010 and *The Gravedigger's Archaeology* (Red Hen Press, 2015), winner of the 2015 Letras Latinas/Red Hen Poetry Prize.

Erika Ayón emigrated from Mexico when she was five years old. She grew up in South Central Los Angeles and graduated from UCLA with a B.A. in English. She was selected as a 2009 PEN Emerging Voices Fellow and has taught poetry to middle and high school students throughout Los Angeles.

Pushcart and Sundress Award nominee, **Danny Baker** arose as an outcast of the 80's L.A. punk rock scene; running wild in the streets. He would move to NYC and create a prolific Wall Street career. Now 45, and extensively published, Danny sits on the Board of the Beyond Baroque Literary Center.

Andres Bermejo is a son of the San Gabriel Valley where he still resides with his wife and two children. He has a BA in Art from California State University, Monterey Bay, and a teaching credential from St. Mary's College. His work also appears in *SPECTRUM*, edited by Don Kingfisher Campbell, and the *Heartbreak Anthology* series, edited by Karineh Mahdessian.

Xochitl-Julisa Bermejo was named the 2013 *Poets & Writers* California Writers Exchange poetry winner. She has work published in *The American Poetry Review, CALYX, The Acentos Review,* and *The Nervous Breakdown* among others. She curates the quarterly reading series HITCHED and is a co-founding member of Women Who Submit.

Laurel Ann Bogen was born in Los Angeles and has lived there her entire life. She is the author of eleven books of poetry and short fiction and is an instructor in the Writers' Program at UCLA Extension.

Jeffrey Bryant is a writer and poet living in Los Angeles. His work has previously appeared in the *L.A. Weekly, Los Angeles Times* and *Poetic Diversity* literary journal.

Ruthie Buell is a teacher and child development expert who has been hosting "Halfway Down the Stairs With Uncle Ruthie" on KPFK-FM radio for fifty-five years. She also has a "Poet Tree," a Chinese elm, in front of her home where anyone can place a poem, a thought, a quote for all to share.

Don Kingfisher Campbell is poetry editor of the *Angel City Review*, editor of the *San Gabriel Valley Poetry Quarterly* and *Spectrum*; host of Saturday Afternoon Poetry in Pasadena; and Creative Writing instructor in the Occidental College Upward Bound Program. He earned his MFA in Creative Writing from Antioch University, Los Angeles. For publishing credits, please go to: dkc1031.blogspot.com.

Jessica M. Wilson Cardenas is a Poet born in East L.A. She has her MFA in Poetry from Otis College of Art and Design and her B.A. in Creative Writing from UC Riverside, and is celebrating 6 years of her founding of the Los Angeles Poet Society, of which she is President. She is a Poet Teacher for California Poets in the Schools and the L.A. County Area Coordinator.

Anaid Carreno was born in Oceanside and moved throughout California and Mexico as a child. Carreno attended California State University of Los Angeles for two years where she was further inspired to write poetry. She received a Bachelor's degree in Sociology and a minor in Chicana/o Studies from Sonoma State University.

Iliana Carter is an actress, writer, and activist. Frustrated with the lack of visibility and quality roles available to women of color in the entertainment industry, she focused on writing to create that content for herself and others like her. Her work aims to represent the richness and diversity of experiences of working-class people of color.

Jessica Ceballos curates Avenue 50 Studio's monthly "Bluebird Reading" as well as the *Poesia Para La Gente* poetry program. She's 1/4 of the experiment in publishing known as Writ Large Press and holds a seat with the Highland Park Neighborhood Council. She also chairs their Arts & Culture Committee. jessicaceballos.com

Adrian Ernesto Cepeda is an L.A. poet who is currently enrolled in the MFA Graduate program at Antioch University in Los Angeles. His poetry has been featured in *The Yellow Chair Review, Thick With Conviction, Silver Birch Press* and one of his poems was named *Cultured Vultures' Top 3 Poems of the Week.* You can connect with Adrian on his website:.adrianernesto-cepeda.com

Angel Cerritos is originally from north Long Beach, CA. He's currently a special education teacher in North Hills, CA, and has found this job to provide him with what he always wanted to be—someone who has the privilege to serve his community.

Robert Chambers is author of *Circumflections Of A Scream* and *Unforgiven.* He appeared in "The United States Of Poetry" on PBS and is a writer of plays on homelessness like "Open Air Gallery" and "The Kindness Of Strangers." A journalist appearing in the L.A. Weekly, and featured in the

Los Angeles Times, among other publications, he is President of the 501 (c) 3 non-profit corporation, the Homeless Writers Coalition in Los Angeles.

Lisa Cheby, a librarian/poet, holds an MFA from Antioch and is an MLIS candidate at SJSU. Her poems and reviews have appeared in various journals and anthologies. Her chapbook, *Love Lessons from Buffy the Vampire Slayer*, is available from Dancing Girl Press. lisacheby.wordpress.com

Gabreal Cho is from the Valley. She and her mother tend to their garden rain or shine.

Chiwan Choi is the author of *The Flood* (Tía Chucha Press, 2010) and *Abductions* (Writ Large Press, 2012). His current projects are *Ghostmaker*, a book he is writing, presenting, and destroying during the course of 2015, and *if 100, then 150*, a poem in 150 parts. Chiwan is also a founding partner at Writ Large Press, a DTLA based indie publisher.

Marcus Clayton grew up in South Gate, CA, and holds an M.F.A. in Poetry from CSU Long Beach. He coordinates poetry reading events in Long Beach, is an assistant poetry editor for *The Offing*, and teaches at Long Beach City College and Fullerton College. He has been published in *Tahoma Literary Review*, *Mason's Road*, *San Pedro River Review*, *Los Angeles Review of Books*, *RipRap Journal*, and *Lipstick Party Magazine*, among others.

Wanda Coleman, born in Watts and raised in South Los Angeles, is considered the "unofficial" poet laureate of the city. She published many books of poetry, fiction, and nonfiction, as well as spoken word CDs, and won numerous awards, including bronze medal finalist for the National Book Award, Lenore Marshall Poetry Prize, and fellowships from the National Endowment for the Arts and the Guggenheim Foundation. She passed away in 2013.

Rafa Cruz is a poet and lyricist from South Gate, California. He dedicates his work to the passion, feeling and emotion of the children of immigrants in Los Angeles, particularly those with whom he shares his culture, generation, time and space.

Iliana Cuellar is a queer Salvadoreña *cumbia* enthusiast born and raised in LA. Her writing explores themes of diaspora, reconciled alienation, and love across borders and binaries.

Yago S. Cura is an Adult Services Librarian at the Vernon branch of the Los Angeles Public Library in sunny South Central Los Angeles. He publishes the poetry, fiction, and prose of authors from *las Américas* in *Hinchas de Poesía* (hinchasdepoesia.com) with Jim Heavily and Jennifer Therieau. Yago's poetry has appeared in *Huizache, KWELI, PALABRA, Borderlands, Lungfull!, COMBO, LIT, U.S. Latino Review, 2nd Avenue, Exquisite Corpse, FIELD,* and *Slope.*

Art Currim lives in Los Angeles, by way of India, the UK, Canada, and Orange County. His work has appeared in *Yay!LA Magazine* and the *San Gabriel Valley Poet's Quarterly.* He has been a featured poet at Dirty Laundry Lit, Bluebird Poetry Series, and A Rose in a Prose (of which he is now co-host).

Kamau Daáood is an iconic figure in Southern California's arts scene. He is a performance poet, educator, and community arts activist widely acknowledged as a driving force behind Los Angeles's black cultural renaissance. Among his many accomplishments, he is cofounder of the World Stage in South L.A.'s Leimert Park

Doren Damico is a freelance writer producing articles and materials on education and parenting issues. Doren currently uses every spare moment to write on her seven volume metaphysical science fiction series.

Carol V. Davis is the author of *Between Storms* (Truman State University Press, 2012). She won the 2007 T.S. Eliot Prize for *Into the Arms of Pushkin: Poems of St. Petersburg.* Twice a Fulbright scholar in Russia, her poetry has been read on NPR, Radio Russia and at the Library of Congress. She teaches at Santa Monica College and Antioch University, Los Angeles. She is a poetry editor of the Los Angeles newspaper the *Jewish Journal.* Recent and forthcoming work in *Mid-American Review, American Review, Crab Orchard Review, Hayden's Ferry Review* and *American Life in Poetry.*

Iris De Anda is a Guanaca Tapatia who hosts The Writers Underground Open Mic at the Eastside Cafe every third Thursday of the month. Author of *CODESWITCH: Fires From Mi Corazón.* irisdeanda.com

Seven Dhar (sevendhar.wordpress.com) is the 2015 winner of the *San Gabriel Valley Poetry Quarterly* chapbook contest, SGV Poetry Festival broadside contest, dual Los Angeles Poet Society National Women's Month acrostic contests, voted Poetrypalooza's poet laureate, appears online and in various anthologies including *LAWS Review* (lawordsalon.com), *The Border Crossed Us* (Vagabond Books), and *Heartbreak II* and *III*. Shabda (Primordial Sound) Press is publishing Seven's forthcoming collection, *Under the Influence (of Eleven Classic Poems)*.

David M. Diaz lives and works in Los Angeles. He recently completed his MFA at Long Beach State, where he also completed his undergrad. His work has been published by *Bird's Thumb Collective*, *Silver Birch Press*, *The San Pedro Review*, *American Mustard*, and *Tiny Splendor Press*.

Kim Dower is the author of three collections of poetry, *Air Kissing on Mars*, *Slice of Moon*, and *Last Train to the Missing Planet*, all from Red Hen Press. Her work has been featured in Garrison Keillor's, "The Writer's Almanac," and Ted Kooser's, "American Life in Poetry," as well as in *Barrow Street*, *Eclipse*, *Los Angeles Review*, *Ploughshares*, and *Rattle*. Her poems are included in the anthology, *Wide Awake: Poets of Los Angeles and Beyond*. She teaches a workshop called, *Poetry and Dreaming* in the B.A. Program of Antioch University. kimdowerpoetry.com

Sharif Dumani is a Los Angeles musician/poet with a bachelor's degree in history from California State University, Northridge. Dumani has worked with musicians such as Cody ChesnuTT, Alice Bag, Silver Apples, Kawabata Makoto (Acid Mothers Temple), and the Tyde just to name a few; as well as writes for his own musical projects: Sex Stains, Exploding Flowers, and Future Shoxxx. In 2014 and 2015, Repel Industries published written work by Dumani in their "Flash No. 1" and "Love Zine" prints.

Christian Elder is a playwright, painter, and filmmaker living in the San Fernando Valley. His poems have appeared in many publications, including *Saturday Afternoon Journal*, *Blue Satellite Magazine*, and *Art/Life* Magazine. His work has been featured on LA radio programs such as KPFK's Poet's Cafe and KXLU's Echo In the Sense.

Seth Elpenor is an obnoxious writer who loves bringing audacious topics like the future of humanity, ecological revolution, and free love into his abrasive prose and the contemporary slime he calls poetry. You can cringe at his 'radical leftist ideas' and total disregard for conventional form by following him @ElpenorS on Twitter.

Francisco Escamilla (Bus Stop Prophet) was born and raised in Boyle heights, East Los Angeles. He started writing at age eight and never stopped. He believes that poetry is medicine. Francisco facilitates poetry workshops in inner city schools, probation camps, and college campuses, locally and internationally.

Yvonne M. Estrada is a poet and photographer. Her chapbook, *My Name on Top of Yours*, is a crown of sonnets about graffiti, accompanied by original photographs. Her poetry has recently appeared in *Lit for Life*, issue 3; *Gutters and Alleyways; Wide Awake: Poets of Los Angeles and Beyond; Talking Writing*, and YAY! LA *Magazine*.

Eric Eztli is an educator, writer, and community organizer from South East Los Angeles. Through his vision and help from community, he has managed to harvest "Alivio Open Mic" from his garage in the city of Bell.

Rich Ferguson is a Pushcart-nominated poet that has shared the stage with Patti Smith, Exene Cervenka, Wanda Coleman, and other esteemed poets and musicians. He has been published in the *Los Angeles Times, Opium*, and his spoken word/music videos have appeared in international film festivals. His poetry collection 8th *& Agony* is out on Punk Hostage Press, and his debut novel, *New Jersey Me*, will be published by Rare Bird Books/Barnacle Books in Summer 2016.

Born and raised in Pacoima (1985-2003), **Mariana Franco** uprooted herself and lived among the Redwood trees of Humboldt County (2003-present) in pursuit of an artist's lifestyle. Currently living a life of travel, leisure, and bliss betwixt the chaotic passion of Los Angeles and the serene solitude of Humboldt County.

Jamie Asaye FitzGerald's poetry has appeared in *Works & Days, Mom Egg Review, Cultural Weekly, Literary Mama* and *Wide Awake: Poets of Los Angeles and Beyond*, among other publications. She received an Academy of American Poets College Prize at the University of Southern California and an MFA in poetry from San Diego State University. Originally from Hawaii, she lives in Los Angeles where she works for Poets & Writers.

Angela Rose Flores is a writer, musician, and songwriter from East Los Angeles. Her writing is profoundly influenced by a passionate love of nature, relationship perspectives, and the awakening of self-discovery.

Michael C. Ford has been publishing since 1970 and credited with over 28 volumes of print documents. He's been featured on 77 spoken word tracks, including 4 solo documents, since 1983. His debut vinyl received a Grammy nomination in 1987 and his Selected Poems earned a Pulitzer nomination in 1998. His CD project, *Look Each Other in the Ears* (Hen House Studios 2014), includes surviving members of The Doors. Amalio Madueño's Ranchos Press in New Mexico published a chapbook-length poem entitled *the driftwood crucifix* (2015). His volume of new work, *Women Under the Influence*, appeared in 2015 from Word Palace Press.

A native of Los Angeles, **Jerry Garcia** is a poet, photographer and filmmaker. His poetry has appeared in a variety of journals and anthologies including: *Askew, The Chiron Review, Palabra, Lummox Journal* and *Wide Awake: Poets of Los Angeles and Beyond*, and his chapbook *Hitchhiking With the Guilty*.

Nikolai Garcia studied creative writing and poetry at East Los Angeles College under Professor Carol Lem. Some of his other work has been featured in online poetry journals like *Chaparral* and *Kuikatl*. He enjoys pizza, coffee, and revolution.

Marisa Urrutia Gedney, born and raised in Los Angeles, was recently named one of *Forbes Magazine*'s top 30 under 30 in Education. She is currently the Director of Education at 826LA where she helps students write and publish their stories.

Dana Gioia is current California Poet Laureate, born and raised in Hawthorne. He has published five books of poetry, most recently *99 Poems: New & Selected* (Graywolf Press, 2016). He won the 2001 American Book Award. He teaches poetry and music at the University of Southern California.

liz gonzález, a fourth generation Southern Californian, lives in Long Beach. Her poetry, fiction, and memoirs have appeared in numerous literary journals, periodicals, and anthologies. lizgonzalez.com

William A. Gonzalez was born in the "other" Los Angeles, California: 90017. His passion for writing began by spraying chemicals on public walls. Painting stories by way of poetry is his favorite hobby.

Dorothy Randall Gray is a certified life coach and best-selling author of *Soul Between The Lines: Freeing Your Creative Spirit Through Writing* (Avon/Harper-Collins, 1998). In addition to six books of poetry, fiction, and nonfiction, her work has appeared in numerous anthologies, periodicals, and theater productions.

Robert Gribbin is 72 years of age and lives in Woodland Hills, CA. In 2008 he won the Editor's Choice Award for Poetry in association with the Los Angeles Community Colleges.

Peter J Harris is author of *The Black Man of Happiness: In Pursuit of My 'Unalienable Right,'* winner of the American Book Award, and *Bless the Ashes* (Tía Chucha Press, 2014), winner of the PEN Oakland Josephine Miles Award. He's a member of the Anansi Writers Workshop at the World Stage in LA's Leimert Park.

Hazel Clayton Harrison's poetry and prose are inspired by the richness and diversity of L.A.'s cultures and by the beauty of Southern California's landscape. Her memoir, *Crossing the River Ohio*, was released in 2014. When not writing poetry, she enjoys traveling and writing social commentary in her blog hazelpearls.blogspot.com.

Kevin Hearle is the author of *Each Thing We Know Is Changed Because We Know It, and Other Poems* (Ahsahta Press of Boise State University). He has taught at numerous universities across California, including Cal State L.A., UCLA Extension, Santa Clara University, and UC Santa Cruz. He was a Visiting Scholar at the Bill Lane Center for the American West at Stanford University from 2008-2013.

Adolfo Hernandez is a Sylmar-based poet, writer, comedian, and saint. He maintains the poetry blog: *Los Brainiacs* at nefariousx.blogspot.com.

Raul Herrera is a member of the Get Lit Players, which utilizes classic poetry and spoken word in a performance troupe of high school students, serving 20,000 teens a year in Los Angeles.

William Ryan Hilary has had poetry and fiction published in several places, including *A Fine Flu* and *Black and White*. He was born in Ireland, raised in London and currently lives in Los Angeles where he is involved with the literary arts center Beyond Baroque.

Marlene Hitt is Southern California born, having lived in her starter house for 56 years. She's had the same husband since 1956. Marlene graduated from Occidental College. Her latest book of poetry is *Clocks and Water Drops* (Moonrise Press). Before that she was published by Arcadia Press in the "Making of America" series with a "popular history," *Sunland-Tujunga From Village to City*.

Jen Hofer is a Los Angeles-based poet, translator, social justice interpreter, teacher, knitter, book-maker, public letter-writer, urban cyclist, and co-founder of the language justice and language experimentation collaborative *Antena* and the local language justice advocacy collective, *Antena Los Angeles*. Her most recent translations are *Intervenir/Intervene* by Mexican writers Dolores Dorantes and Rodrigo Flores Sánchez (Ugly Duckling Presse, 2015) and *Estilo/Style* by Dolores Dorantes (Kenning Editions, forthcoming 2016).

Alexandra Hohmann is a high school English teacher and current facilitator of In The Words of Womyn (ITWOW), a women's writing circle, in Sylmar, CA. Hohmann has been published in *Yay!LA* magazine (online) and the *San Gabriel Valley Quarterly*. She is working on a follow up to her self-published chapbook, *Wild Heart* (2013).

Boris Salvador Ingles at his core bleeds Los Angeles. Born and raised in Boyle Heights, he finds beauty and soul in every facet of life. Boris combines poetry and photography as means for visual and emotional expression. A mixture of humor, rawness, vulnerability, and a sense for dark street realism.

Gerda Govine Ituarte, Ed.D. is author of *Oh, Where is My Candle Hat?* (2012) and *Alterations/Thread Light Through Eye of Storm* (2015). Her work has appeared in *The Altadena Poetry Review Anthology 2015, Spectrum, San Gabriel Valley Poetry Quarterly*; online publications *Dryland Los Angeles Arts and Letters, Hometown Pasadena, Ms. Aligned*; and *Frontera Esquina Magazine* in Tijuana. She read at Lit Crawl L.A., 2012-2015, Avenue 50 Studio, The World Stage, Holy Grounds; The Coffee Gallery Backstage; and in Canada, Colombia, Cuba and Mexico.

traci kato-kiriyama is a third generation LA native/Nikkei, queer, writer, actor, devised theatre practitioner, educator, and community organizer. She is the Director/Co-Founder of Tuesday Night Project, presenter of Tuesday Night Café—established in 1998 and the oldest, still-running, Asian American free mic series in the country. She and aerialist/actor Kennedy Kabasares make up the award-winning PULL project ensemble, currently developing their show PULL: Tales of Clamor, while she finishes her second book of poetry and writing, slated for release by Writ Large Press in 2016.

Douglas Kearney is the author of several collections, including *Mess and Mess and* (Noemi, 2015), *Patter* (Red Hen Press, 2014), and *The Black Automaton* (Fence Books, 2009). He was born in Brooklyn and raised in Altadena, CA. He lives in Santa Clarita and teaches at CalArts.

Karen Kevorkian has published poetry collections with What Books Press and Red Hen Press. Her poems have appeared in *Antioch Review, Michigan Quarterly Review, Denver Quarterly,* and the California journals *Volt, Pool, Spillway, Poetry Flash,* and *Poetry International.* She teaches at UCLA.

Doug Knott is the author of the collection *Small Dogs Bark Cartoons* (Seven Wolves, 1991), various chapbooks, and is included in the *Outlaw Bible of American Poetry* (Thunder Mouth's Press, 1999). He was a member of the seminal poetry performance troupe "The Carma Bums," created poetry videos which played on broadcast TV, and since 2013 has been president of the board of trustees of Beyond Baroque Literary Arts Foundation.

Haley Laningham is currently a student at Pepperdine University majoring in Creative Writing and Hispanic Studies. She spent her childhood in many different places including Boston, Massachusetts, and Fresno, California, but now calls Los Angeles her deeply-loved home. She hopes her poetry demonstrates the diverse experiences she has collected, as well as brings voice to unspoken American histories and journeys.

Teka Lark is the BlkGrrrl Show host & producer, a KPFK Feminist Magazine producer, a KChung DJ, BlkGrrrl Book Fair founder, *LA Weekly* contributor, freelance journalist and poet. Find her online with the #BlkGrrrl hashtag.

Anthony A. Lee, Ph.D., lives in Los Angeles and teaches history at UCLA and at West Los Angeles College. His most recent book of poetry translations is *Love Is My Savior: The Arabic Poems of Rumi* (Michigan State University Press, 2016).

Janice Lee is the author of *Kerotakis* (Dog Horn Press, 2010), *Daughter* (Jaded Ibis, 2011), *Damnation* (Penny-Ante Editions, 2013), *Reconsolidation: Or, it's the ghosts who will answer you* (Penny-Ante Editions, 2015), and *The Sky Isn't Blue* (Civil Coping Mechanisms, forthcoming 2016). She currently lives in Los Angeles where she is Editor of the #RECURRENT Novel Series for Jaded Ibis Press, Assistant Editor at *Fanzine*, Executive Editor at *Entropy*, and Founder/CEO of POTG Design. She can be found online at janicel.com.

Kimberly Lieu was born and raised in Southern California. She earned her BA in English Literature from San Francisco State University and has spent most of her adult life traveling and living in different parts of the continent. Staying in a small village on Lake Atitlan, Guatemala inspired her book of word portraits, *agridulce(bittersweet)* (ILOANBooks, 2012). More poems can be found in *San Francisco Peace and Hope Literary Journal*.

Mark Lipman, recipient of the 2015 Joe Hill Labor Poetry Award; founder of VAGABOND; a writer, poet, multi-media artist, and activist, is the author of six books, most recently, *Poetry for the Masses*; and *Global Economic Amnesty*. Co-founder of the *Berkeley Stop the War Coalition* (USA), *Agir Contre la Guerre* (France) and *Occupy Los Angeles*. Currently, he is a member of POWER (People Organized for Westside Renewal), *Occupy Venice*, the *Revolutionary Poets Brigade, 100 Thousand Poets for Change* and the *International Workers of the World* (IWW). vagabondbooks.net

Jaime Lopez is a comedian and writer who lives in Los Angeles.

Phoebe MacAdams was born and raised in New York City, but has lived in California most of her adult life. In 1986, she moved to Los Angeles where she taught English and Creative Writing at Roosevelt High School until her retirement in 2011. She is a founding member of Cahuenga Press. Her books of poetry include: *Sunday* (Tombouctou Press, 1983), *Ordinary Snake Dance* (Cahuenga Press, 1994), *Livelihood,* (Cahuenga Press, 2003), *Strange Grace* (Cahuenga Press, 2007), and *Touching Stone* (Cahuenga Press, 2012).

Robert Mäder-Kammer was born in Germany in 1949 and came to the U.S. in 1956 with his mother and younger brother. He is a retired Master Sergeant, a grandfather, a graduate of Whittier College and has an MS in clinical counseling. He lives with his artist wife, two dogs and five feral cats on 20 desert acres in Roosevelt, east of Lancaster, CA.

Karineh Mahdessian hosts *La Palabra* and co-facilitates *Las Lunas Locas*. She writes. She loves. She rights. She eats. She rites. She breathes.

Ruthie Marlenée, with roots in the Tequila country of Jalisco, lives in the San Fernando Valley. She has earned a Writer's Certificate with Distinction from UCLA and has been nominated for a Kirkwood Literary Award. She is a published novelist and short story writer, screenwriter, and former student of Suzanne Lummis.

Jeffrey Martin is a poet, storyteller, author of four poetry books, three children's books, and a play. His first book, *Weapon of Choice*, won the 2008 Best Book of Poetry of the New Jersey Beach Book Festival and honorable mentions in the New York and London book festivals. The poetry book, *As Sons Love Their Mothers*, and his children's book, *Silly Billy*, received honorable mentions in the 2011 San Francisco Book Festival.

Rubén Martínez is a writer, teacher, and performer. He is Fletcher Jones Chair in Literature and Writing at Loyola Marymount University and the author of several books, including *Crossing Over* and *Desert America*.

Rhiannon McGavin is a teenage writer who was born and raised in Los Angeles. Trained in Shakespeare, she uses her performance skills for everything from producing online videos on *TheGeekyBlonde* to opening local protests with poems.

elena minor is the author of *TITULADA* (Noemi Press, 2014). Her work in poetry and prose has been published in more than two dozen literary journals and anthologized in *Angels of the Americlypse: An Anthology of New Latin@ Writing* (Counterpath Press, 2014) and *Best American Experimental Writing of 2015* (Omnidawn Publishing). She is a recipient of the Chicano/Latino Literary Prize and founding editor of *PALABRA*.

Penelope Moffet is a poet and painter who lives in the Los Angeles area. Her poems have appeared in *The Missouri Review, Columbia, The Broome Review, Permafrost, Pearl, Steam Ticket, The MacGuffin, Riverwind* and other magazines. She has published one poetry collection, *Keeping Still* (Dorland Mountain Arts Colony, 1995), and her work was included in *What Wildness Is This: Women Write About the Southwest* (University of Texas Press, 2007) and *Spectrum: 140 SoCal Poets* (2015).

Bill Mohr's collections of poetry include *Hidden Proofs* (Bombshelter Press, 1982), *Bittersweet Kaleidoscope* (2006), and a bilingual selection of poems from both of those books, *Pruebas Ocultas* (Bonobos Editores, Mexico, 2015). He also has an account of West Coast poetry, *Holdouts: The Los Angeles Poetry Renaissance 1948-1992* (2011, University of Iowa Press). He has edited or co-edited three anthologies of Los Angeles or West Coast poets. After years of working as a typesetter, Mohr returned to school, got a Ph.D. in Literature from UCSD in 2004, and has lived in Long Beach and taught at CSULB since 2006.

Alejandro Molina has an MFA in Theatre (California State University Northridge, 2010) and Teacher Education Degree (Mexico). He is a poet, mime, actor, director, and playwright: Vivepez.wordpress.com and mimosbinbon.wordpress.com.

Henry J. Morro is the author of the poetry collection *Corpses of Angels* (Bombshelter Press). His poetry has been published in *Seneca Review, New Letters, Black Warrior Review, Poet Lore, Askew, Chiron Review, California Quarterly,* and *Sonora Review.*

Sybil Mosely was born at the California Hospital Downtown and grew up in the vibrant cultural diversity of Pico-Fairfax, Mid-Wilshire, Venice, and East Hollywood.

Majid Naficy, the Arthur Rimbaud of Persian poetry, fled Iran in 1983, a year and a half after the execution of his wife Ezzat in Tehran. He has been living in Venice Beach and Santa Monica since May 1984. He has published two collections of poetry *Muddy Shoes* (Beyond Baroque, 1999) and *Father and Son* (Red Hen Press, 2003) as well as his doctoral dissertation *Modernism and Ideology in Persian Literature* (University Press of America, 1997) in English.

Janet Nippell grew up in North Hollywood and now lives in Pasadena. She wrote *Mostly on Foot: A Year in L.A.* with Ben Yandell and has had poems in *Rattle*, *A Narrow Fellow*, and *Altadena Poetry Review*.

Born in Amarillo, Texas, raised in Sidney, Nebraska, **Harry E. Northup** has lived in Los Angeles since 1968. Harry has made a living as an actor for 34 years, acting in 37 films, including "Taxi Driver" and "The Silence of the Lambs." Northup has had 11 poetry books published, the latest one being *East Hollywood: Memorial To Reason* (Cahuenga Press, 2015).

Martin Ott has lived in Los Angeles for twenty years and is the author of six books of poetry and fiction, including the poetry book *Underdays* (Sandeen Prize winner, University of Notre Dame Press, 2015), and the short story collection *Interrogations* (Fomite Press). More at martinottwriter.com.

Melinda Palacio is a Tía Chucha Press poet and writes a bimonthly column for *La Bloga*. Her work has been published in a variety of anthologies and journals, including the Academy of American Poets 2015 poem-a-day program. She is the author of the novel, *Ocotillo Dreams* (Bilingual Review Press, 2011), and the poetry collections *Folsom Lockdown* (Kulupi Press, 2009) and *How Fire Is a Story, Waiting* (Tía Chucha Press, 2012).

Rae Paris is from Carson, California. She is a NEA Fellow whose writing appears or is forthcoming in *Outpost19*, *Women: A Cultural Review*, *Transition Magazine*, *Guernica*, *The Common*, *Solstice*, *Hobart Pulp*, *Dismantle*, and many others. Her poem "The Forgetting Tree" was selected as Best of the Net 2013. A Pushcart Prize nominee, her work has been supported by The Helene Wurlitzer Foundation, Hambidge, Atlantic Center for the Arts, and VONA. She lives and writes mostly in East Lansing, Michigan where she's Assistant Professor of Creative Writing at Michigan State University.

Candace Pearson's poems play with the psychology of landscape. Her book, *Hour of Unfolding*, won the Liam Rector First Book Prize for Poetry from Longwood University, and her poems and reviews have been published in fine journals and anthologies nationwide.

Alice Pero's first book of poetry, *Thawed Stars* (Sun Ink, 1999), was hailed by Kenneth Koch as having "clarity and surprises." Pero has taught poetry to grade school children for 24 years on both coasts. She has lived in Los

Angeles for 20 years and founded the long-running Moonday reading series. She is also an accomplished flutist.

Ramona Pilar is currently working on a collection of essays entitled *Darth Vader Abandoned his Daughter and Other Thoughts Along The Heroine's Journey*. She creates and leads pop-culture myth-based creative writing workshops, has a B.A. in Film and Cultural Representation from UC Davis and an MFA in Creative Writing from Antioch University, Los Angeles. She can occasionally be found troubadouring with her band The Raveens. Peruse her life's work at RamonaPilar.com.

Jenuine Poetess is a writer and artist, founder of Waco Poets Society and ITWOW International—a womyn's writing circle project. She organizes and creates rooted in the fierce conviction that empowering creative health is a matter of justice. Jenuine is a former Los Angeles resident who lives in Central Texas where she practices finding artful ways to disrupt the homeostasis of her city.

Holly Prado has had eleven books published. Her work has also appeared in literary magazines and anthologies since the early 1970s. Recent poems are in the new 2015 anthology *Wide Awake: Poets of Los Angeles and Beyond*, edited by Suzanne Lummis, Pacific Coast Series, Beyond Baroque.

Wanting to be seen in his youth, **Arturo Quiros** started rhyming in ciphers at the age of 16. Off the top, his word play often depicted the fear and the reality of a kid growing up in underserved communities of color. Learning to walk with what he carries, Art utilizes his love for words to share his story and invites listeners to do the same.

A. Razor is a poet and storyteller who has been raised in Southern California/Aztlan and whose work is infused with his multicultural experiences that range from living on a desert indigenous reservation to the inner city of Los Angeles. He has led a marginalized life for the most part, surviving everything from homelessness, addiction and incarceration to continue to create his body of work. In 2012 he co-founded Punk Hostage Press with Iris Berry in Los Angeles, as well as the creative writing outreach organization Words As Works in 2013.

ellen reich teaches creative writing and autobiography for Santa Monica College's Emeritus Program. Her latest book was published in 2015 by Tebot Bach Press entitled "Sacrifices Have To Be Human."

Steven Reigns is a Los Angeles-based poet and educator, appointed as the first City Poet of West Hollywood in October of 2014. Alongside over a dozen chapbooks, he has published the collections *Inheritance* (Sibling Rivalry, 2011) and *Your Dead Body is My Welcome Mat* (Burning Page Press, 2001). He edited My Life is Poetry, featuring his students in the first-ever autobiographical poetry workshop for LGBT seniors, and has taught writing workshops around the country to LGBT youth and people living with HIV. Visit him at stevenreigns.com.

Luivette Resto was born in Aguas Buenas, Puerto Rico but proudly raised in the Bronx. Her first book of poetry, *Unfinished Portrait* (Tía Chucha Press, 2008), was named a finalist for the 2009 Paterson Poetry Prize. She has served as a contributing poetry editor for *Kweli Journal*, is a CantoMundo fellow and member of the Con Tinta advisory board. Her new book, *Ascension* (Tía Chucha Press, 2013), was recently selected for the 2014 Paterson Award for Literary Excellence for previous finalists of the Paterson Poetry Prize. Some of her latest work appears in *Luna Luna Magazine*, *Toe Good Poetry*, and the *Altadena Anthology 2015*. She now lives in the Los Angeles area.

Born in Los Altos de Jalisco, Mexico, **Erika Reyes** grew up in South East Los Angeles and the San Gabriel Valley. She holds two degrees and has traveled many countries to acquire knowledge from the world's diversity.

Michael Reyes is a Chicano poet and arts and culture journalist from Del Rey. A recent graduate from UCLA with degrees in English and Chicana/o Studies, he's mentored and taught writing to pushed-out high school students and researched the significance of in-school creative writing programs.

Thelma T. Reyna is the award-winning author of 4 books: a short story collection (*The Heavens Weep for Us and Other Stories*), 2 poetry chapbooks (*Breath & Bone*; and *Hearts in Common*); and a full-length collection of poetry, *Rising, Falling, All of Us*. Her fifth book, the *Altadena Poetry Review: Anthology 2015*, is a compilation of 105 poems by 60 Southern California poets which she edited and published under her indie imprint, Golden Foothills Press. Thelma is Poet Laureate of the Altadena Library District.

Sophia Rivera is a Chicana writer, educator, and *luna loca* from the womyn's writing circle based in El Sereno, California, *Las Lunas Locas*. Born and raised in Northwest Pasadena, she is also the founder of *Palabras de Pasadena*, a community storytelling and literary project. She believes in the sacred power of telling stories and that poetry saves lives.

Claudia Rodríguez is a writer/performer from Compton, who received her MFA in creative writing from the California Institute of the Arts (CalArts). Her first collection of poetry, *Everybody's Bread*, was published with Korima Press (2015). Most recently, Claudia is a recipient of a "COLA Grant" from the City of Los Angeles Department of Cultural Affairs.

Daniela Rodriguez is a senior at Sylmar High School. She was born in Mexico and immigrated to the United States at three years old. She has been interested in reading, writing, and drawing ever since.

Norma Rodriguez, a native of Porterville, California is the proud daughter of immigrants. She received her Bachelors of Studio Art degree from University of California, Irvine and her Master's of Arts in Latin American studies. She has recently made her home in Los Angeles and loves to read the books, write the poems, paint the art, and love the life.

Ramiro D. Rodriguez was born in Bellflower, California and raised in the Humboldt Park neighborhood of Chicago. Affected by gang life, Ramiro served thirteen-and-a-half years in prison and was released in July 2010. Now living in the San Fernando Valley, he has been active in gang prevention and intervention, youth empowerment projects and community organizing. Ramiro self-published his first chapbook, *Coming Home*.

Trini Rodriguez (Matriz) has been active all her adult life to align the world to it's most caring and sustainable possibilities. She helped found and shares leadership for the community-fostering Tía Chucha's Centro Cultural & Bookstore. Deeply concerned about women's devalued condition, she also holds sacred space for women to heal and become their most authentic selves.

Jeff Rogers grew up in Michigan college towns, including East Lansing. Jeff drove cross country to Los Angeles in 1983, fell in love with it and has lived here ever since. He believes that effing the ineffable is one of the key tasks of poetry and you can find more of his work at lefthandedjeff.com.

Conrad Romo is the producer/host of the literary variety show Tongue & Groove. He is also a co-founder of the NoHo Litcrawl. He has studied writing with Lynda Barry and Jack Grapes. He's been published in *Los Angeles Review*, *Latinos in Lotusland*, *Literature for Life*, *Huizache* and elsewhere. conradromo.com

Jessica Romoff is a member of the Get Lit Players, an award winning Classic teen poetry troupe, comprised of Los Angeles County teenagers.

Melissa Roxas is a poet, human rights activist, and community organizer working for social justice for over twenty years. Melissa is a survivor of abduction and torture by the Philippine military during one of her medical missions in the Philippines in 2009. A Kundiman, PEN USA Emerging Voices, and Great Leap Collaboratory fellow, her work has been published in *RHINO*, *Boxcar Poetry*, *Solo Novo*, and in the anthology "Wide Awake: Poets of Los Angeles and Beyond."

Pogo Saito is the hybrid offspring of Idaho pioneering stock with Japanese American internment camp survivors, raised by drag queens in the wilds of Idaho. So she naturally became a storyteller; she tours with the acclaimed storytelling troupe *We Tell Stories* and is an associate artist with Theatre Movement Bazaar. She was a student of the first Japanese American poet laureate, Lawson Fusao Inada, and is still greatly influenced by his rhythmic prose.

Abel Salas, a journalist and poet based in Boyle Heights, is the publisher and editor of *Brooklyn & Boyle*, a monthly community arts paper. His poems have appeared in *Zyzzyva*, *Huizache*, *Beltway Poetry Quarterly* and the SF State literary journal *Cipactli*, among others. He has shared poetry at festivals in Havana, Cuba; Mexico D.F.; Ajalpan, Puebla; Tijuana, Baja California; and in venues across the U.S. Southwest. As a journalist, Salas has written for *The New York Times*, *Los Angeles Times Magazine*, *LA Weekly*, *Los Angeles Magazine*, *The Austin Chronicle*, and other newspapers, magazines, and periodicals.

Cathie Sandstrom's poems have appeared in *Ploughshares, Runes, Lyric, Solo, Comstock Review, Cider Press Review, Malpais Review, ART/LIFE, Ekphrasis, New Plains Review* among others. Anthologies include *Wide Awake: Poets of Los Angeles and Beyond, Beyond the Lyric Moment, Vincent van Go-Gogh, Open Windows, Blue Arc West,* and *So Luminous the Wildflowers.*

Alejandra Sanchez's work has been featured in the independent film, *I Stare At You and Dream*, KPFK's *Pacifica Radio*, Radio Sombra's *Red Feminist Radio*, Mujeres De Maiz, La Bloga, UCLA *Young Writers Anthology, Hinchas de Poesia*, Duende Literary Journal, *Latino/a Rising: An Anthology of Speculative Fiction* and PBS Newshour's *Where Poetry Lives*. She earned an MFA in Creative Writing at Antioch University, Los Angeles.

Nicky Sa-eun Schildkraut is a poet who teaches literature and creative writing in Los Angeles. She holds an M.F.A. degree in poetry from the University of Florida and a Ph.D. degree in Literature & Creative Writing from the University of Southern California. Her first book of poetry, *Magnetic Refrain*, was published in February 2013 by Kaya Press and she is currently working on a literary novel, *Missing Persons*.

T Sarmina is a xicanx, a queer poet/a, and writer of songs they sang to stray kittens when they were growing up in the Central Valley. Their work focuses on liminality: the liminal spaces we collect memories from, like inside a mother's womb, or the spaces between fiction and nonfiction. Their words are rooted in the landscapes of a California Central Valley in drought.

S. Pearl Sharp has produced the poetry with jazz CDs *Higher Ground* and *On The Sharp Side*; a documentary film on poet Kamau Daáood, *Life Is A Saxophone*; and the poetry performance programs *Mixed Media Poems* and *Typing In The Dark*. Non-fiction books include *The Evening News—Essays and Commentaries from NPR and Other Clouds* and *Black Women for Beginners*. spearlsharp.com

Mahtem Shiferraw is a writer and visual artist who grew up in Eritrea & Ethiopia. Her work has been published in *The 2River View, Cactus Heart Press, Blood Lotus Literary Journal, Luna Luna Magazine, Mandala Literary Journal, Blackberry: A Magazine, Diverse Voices Quarterly, The Bitter Oleander Press, Callaloo Literary Journal*, and elsewhere. She won the Sillerman Prize for African Poets and her full length poetry collection, *Fuchsia*, forthcoming from University of Nebraska Press. Her poetry chapbook, *Behind Walls & Glass*, is forthcoming from Finishing Line Press. She holds an MFA in Creative Writing from Vermont College of Fine Arts.

Mike Sonksen (Mike the Poet) is a third-generation L.A. native acclaimed for poetry performances, published articles, and mentoring teen writers. Following his graduation from UCLA in 1997, he has published over 500 essays and poems. His KCET column "L.A. Letters" celebrates literary Los Angeles.

Robert Stanley was a teacher in the Los Angeles Unified School District, now retired.

Austin Straus is a Brooklyn-born artist and poet, married to the late Wanda Coleman, and with Wanda host of "The Poetry Connexion" on KPFK-FM radio for 15 years. He has lived in Southern California since 1978. He has two poetry collections with Red Hen Press: *Drunk with Light* (2002) and *Intensifications* (2010). A book of love poems by Austin and Wanda, *The Love Project: A Marriage Made in Poetry*, appeared in 2014 by Red Hen Press.

Ambika Talwar is an India-born educator, author, artist, and wellness consultant whose ecstatic style makes her poetry a "bridge to other worlds." She has authored *Creative Resonance: Poetry—Elegant Play, Elegant Change; 4 Stars & 25 Roses;* and chapbooks. She is published in journals and has won an award for a short film. She lives in Los Angeles. Her websites are creativeinfinities.com and goldenmatrixvisions.com.

Tezozomoc is a Los Angeles Chicano Poet and 2009 Oscar-nominated activist. He has been published in the following journals: *CrazyQuilt* (San Diego, CA), *Rhino* (Chicago, IL), *Mind Matters Review* (Silver Spring, MD), *Left Curve* (Oakland, CA), *Next Phase* (Parker, Co.), *Minotaur Press* (San Francisco, CA), *San Fernando Poetry Journal* (San Fernando CA), *Caffeine, Orchard* (Santa Cruz, CA), *Poet's Sanctuary* (Washington), *Black Buzzard Press* (Virginia), *Dance of the Iguana, The Americas Review, LaHoja, Louder Than Bombs, Orale!, Tight* (Guerneville, CA), *(Untitled)* (Southgate California), and *ChupaRosa Writer's '93* calendar. Tezozomoc is also a Huffington Post blogger under huffingtonpost.com/tezozomoc where he blogs about activism and food issues.

Lynne Thompson has authored two full-length poetry collections, *Beg No Pardon* and *Start With A Small Guitar*, as well as three chapbooks. Widely published and anthologized, Thompson received a City of Los Angeles Fellowship in 2015 and serves as the reviews and essays editor of the literary journal, *Spillway*.

Born and raised in Pomona, California, **Michael Torres'** work has appeared in *Okey-Panky, Solo Press, Miramar,* and other journals. Currently, he is an MFA candidate at Minnesota State University, Mankato, where he teaches creative writing and works on *Blue Earth Review.*

Anna Ureña is a Mexican-American writer, poet, and social activist born, raised, and based in South Central Los Angeles. She is the host of a literary podcast *Another Voice From The Crowd* and the editor-in-chief of DRY-LAND. Find her on annaurena.com.

Amy Uyematsu is a sansei (third-generation Japanese American) poet and teacher from Los Angeles. She has four published collections: *30 Miles from J-Town* (Story Line Press,1992), *Nights of Fire, Nights of Rain* (Story Line Press, 1989), *Stone Bow Prayer* (Copper Canyon Press, 2015), and *The Yellow Door* (Red Hen Press, 2015).

Rolland Vasin, pen name Vachine, is a third-generation American writer published in the journals *Open Minds Quarterly, Gnome,* and *Found and Lost.* He is an active open-mic reader at venues from Cambridge, Massachusetts to Big Sur, California. He has featured at Los Angeles' World Stage, The Rapp Saloon, and Cobalt Cafe, among others, and dabbles in improvisational theater and stand-up comedy. The Laugh Factory recognized him as the third funniest CPA in Los Angeles.

GusTavo Adolfo Guerra Vásquez is a multi-disciplinary artist born in Guatemala City and raised both (t)here and in LosT Ángeles, California. GusTavo currently works with young people in their struggle for social justice and uses art as a method of raising consciousness within different communities. He is also working diligently on being a good father to Guillermo, a budding "chapicano" artist.

Vickie Vertiz's essays and poetry can be found in the *Los Angeles Review of Books, The Offing,* the *James Franco Review, KCET Departures,* and in *Open the Door* (McSweeney's and the Poetry Foundation). She was a finalist for the Gabriela Mistral Poetry Prize from the *Cobalt Review* in 2014 and was the Lucille Clifton Scholar at the Community of Writers at Squaw Valley in 2015. She is at work on a memoir about her education titled: *Smart: Growing up Gifted and Brown in Southeast Los Angeles.*

Jennifer Lisa Vest, Ph.D. is a poet, philosopher, and healer of mixed (Black/Native/German) heritage.

Born and raised in Los Angeles, **Estela Victoria-Cordero** moved to Mexico when she was 13, where she turned fiercely to writing upon the illness and subsequent death of her mother, nursed her sister through brain cancer, and was a child survivor of alcoholism, which her father eventually succumbed. While homeless, she applied to USC where she graduated with Honors with a degree in Dental Hygiene in 1994. She is a married mother of four children, and has been with her high school sweetheart, Dr. Franklin Cordero, for thirty years.

Antonieta Villamil is an international award-winning bilingual poet, writer, singer, and editor with over 11 published books. The Cervantes Institute of New York and Literacy Now awarded her the "14 International Latino Book Award, Best Book of Poetry," and she won the "2001 International Poetry Award Gastón Baquero" in Spain. She directs the review and salon *Poesía Féstival* that brings poetry to the underserved community of native Spanish speakers in Los Angeles. antonietavillamil.blogspot.com

Celia Viramontes was born and raised in East Los Angeles, California, the youngest daughter of Mexican immigrant parents. She is a researcher and writer whose policy research on immigrant civic engagement, Proposition 227, and language policy in California has been published in numerous academic journals and books. She is researching and writing the transnational stories of Mexican migrant workers and their families.

Melora Walters' poetry has been published by Writ Large Press, Finishing Line Press, DRYLAND, Enclave/CCM-Entropy, and Serpentine Press. Her art has been shown in Los Angeles, New York, and Berlin.

Hilda Weiss is co-founder and curator for Poetry.LA, a website featuring videos of poets and poetry venues in Southern California. Her chapbook, "Optimism About Trees," was nominated for a Pushcart Prize in 2011. Her poetry has been published in *Askew, Ekphrasis, Poemeleon, Rattle,* and *Salamander,* among others.

Sammy Winston, beloved musician and poet, died on the Fourth of July in 2015 saving lives in an apartment fire in Echo Park. R.I.P. Sammy.

Terry Wolverton is the author of 10 books of poetry, fiction and creative nonfiction, including EMBERS, a novel in poems. She's the founder of Writers At Work, a creative writing studio in Los Angeles, and Affiliate Faculty for the MFA Writing Program at Antioch University Los Angeles.

Nancy Lynée Woo is a 2015 PEN Center USA Emerging Voices Fellow and founding editor of Lucid Moose Lit. She is currently working on a collection of poems about her mixed heritage, called *The Great Divide*. Often caught cavorting around Long Beach, CA, she can also be found at nancylyneewoo.com.

Gail Wronsky is the author or coauthor of eleven books of poetry and prose. She lives in Topanga Canyon.

Born of Los Angeles, **Tina Yang** grew up on the Northern California monastery grounds where her mother became a Buddhist nun in 1987. Tina holds a BA in Film Studies from UCLA, and attended UCLA Extension's Writers' Program where she studied with poet noir Suzanne Lummis. Currently Tina is enrolled at Poets At Work with Terry Wolverton and is working on her first chapbook which will be published by Arroyo Seco Press in early 2016. She can be found online at tinylilobserver.weebly.com.

Mariano Zaro is the author of four bilingual poetry books, most recenty *The House of Mae Rim/La casa de Mae Rim* (Carayan Press, 2008) and *Tres letras/Three Letters* (Walrus/Morsa, 2012). Zaro's poems are included in *Wide Awake* (Pacific Coast Poetry Series, 2015) and *Monster Verse* (Penguin Random House, 2015). He has translated American poets Tony Barnstone, Philomene Long, and Sarah Maclay. He teaches Spanish for Heritage Speakers at Rio Hondo College (Whittier, CA). marianozaro.com.